Outdoor Learning and Play
Ages 8-12

Kathleen Glascott Burriss
Barbara Foulks Boyd

Editors

Association for
Childhood Education International
17904 Georgia Ave., Ste. 215, Olney, MD 20832
800-423-3563 • www.acei.org

Bruce Herzig, ACEI Editor
Anne Bauer, ACEI Editor
Deborah Jordan Kravitz, Design and Production

Library of Congress Cataloging-in-Publication Data
Outdoor learning and play, ages 8-12 / Kathleen Glascott Burriss and Barbara Foulks
Boyd, editors.
      p. cm.
  Includes bibliographical references.
  ISBN 0-87173-165-7 (pbk.)
1. Outdoor education. 2. Outdoor recreation for children. 3. Recesses. I. Burriss,
Kathleen Glascott. II. Boyd, Barbara Foulks.

  LB1047.099 2005
  372.13'84--dc22

                                                                                        20040122197

Dedication

We dedicate this book to our husbands, who provide a steadying influence in our lives.

I dedicate this work to Larry, my husband and best friend, who reminds me that when I do not have time to play that I am doing too much. He balances me to take time to enjoy the out-of-doors, which energizes the body, stimulates the mind, and soothes the heart.

—Kathy

I dedicate this work to Calvin, also my husband and best friend, who is attuned to the outdoor environment and lives in the moment. He revels in the beauty and equilibrium of nature, reminding me to do the same.

—Barbara

Special acknowledgment goes to Dr. Tracey Ring for helping create quality outdoor environments for the children at the Homer Pittard Campus School in Murfreesboro, Tennessee. We also thank Lee Yonda, 5th-grade teacher at Filmore Elementary, Filmore, New York, who photographed her children having fun in the snow. And finally, thanks to Ken Robinson and Larry Burriss, whose photographs throughout the book tell the important story of outdoor learning and play.

A Note to Readers . . .

Many current societal trends devalue out-of-door experiences for older children. Therefore, classroom teachers and practitioners are required to provide additional justification to extend learning activities to the out-of-doors.

This book affords educators with a rationale for elementary and middle school children's outdoor learning and play activities. In order to maximize opportunities for children's intellectual, social, and emotional learning in the outdoors, this collection of articles provides teachers with both the explanation, the "why," and the strategies, the "how," for planning quality outdoor experiences.

One of our many concerns is that with limited outside experience, children themselves will fail to regard the value of the out-of-doors as an environment. Teachers report children no longer know what to do when taken out-of-doors. Puddles, grassy fields, and snow piles no longer serve as catalysts for curiosity and exploration. In fact, teachers also say some children decline the opportunity to go outside because they consider it hot, cold, or boring. As children lose their interest in and fondness for the out-of-doors, they also may lose their respect for its importance and regard for its value.

This book includes a collection of writings that will enable classroom teachers and other adults who work with children to effectively plan learning and play opportunities in the out-of-doors. The first section provides a historical foundation for outdoor play and learning, a rationale for understanding different physical environments and playscapes, and guidelines for the inclusion of populations with special needs in the out-of-doors. Section II provides a developmental framework for justifying elementary and middle school children's outdoor activities. Chapters address the relationship between the out-of-doors and children's developmental stages, the role of recess in children's social and emotional development, and the possibility of community and conflict resolution. Chapters in Section III describe both the potential and practicality of using the outdoors as a classroom for studying the sciences, social studies, arts, and geography curricula.

Experts in their respective fields were invited to write chapters to support particular content areas. In order to establish a general foundation for understanding the contributions of outdoor activities for elementary and middle school children's learning and development, the reader is encouraged to consider the book as a total unit. However, the authors realize that teachers have individual needs and concerns regarding the out-of-doors. In this case, each section targets an overriding principle, including theoretical and historical foundations, developmental issues, and curriculum integration.

—Kathleen G. Burriss and
Barbara Foulks Boyd

Table of Contents

Introduction

Joe L. Frost

Joe L. Frost is the Parker Centennial
Professor Emeritus at the University of
Texas at Austin.

Through reminiscing about my childhood play during the Depression era in the Ouachita Mountains of Arkansas and by studying children at play throughout my adult life, I have come to believe that many contemporary children are not merely deprived of play but are essentially deprived of the healthiest and richest forms of play. The richest forms are described by children as the most fun, the most exciting, the most interesting, and by theorists and writers as "deep play" (Ackerman, 1999), "flow" (Csikszentmihalyi, 1990), and "self-actualizing" (Maslow, 1962). The common denominator of these explanations is play that is transcendental—play in which the child loses contact with the outside world, places herself into mental oneness with the activity, loses inhibitions, revels in physical risk and mental challenge, and creates a miniature world of magic and intrigue. In so doing, the child rises above or transcends ordinary limits of play and becomes one with the social and environmental milieu.

Transcendental play is perhaps understood only to those who experience such phenomena as children. Adults who reflect back upon their personal childhood memories may recall such special play as having a sense of timelessness, and being characterized by risk, obsession, ecstasy, and intense mental states. The senses are heightened, consciousness is narrowed, self-consciousness disappears, and the person becomes absolutely absorbed in the activity. I suspect that those who would deprive children of free play, recess, and the fundamental right to play are those who themselves missed, or fail to understand, the deep significance of such play to children's development.

My earliest recollection of transcendental play dates to my primary school days, when traditional games and free, contrived play filled our recess periods. A small stream ran out of the nearby woods and across the schoolyard, gaining vigor and intrigue following rains. Pulling off shoes and rolling up pants, we waded in and built dams of mud to capture large expanses of water. A rival group, catching the excitement, built a dam upstream and eventually let the water loose in torrents to wash out our downstream dam. This led to frantic activity and collaborative schemes to ultimately build a dam from rocks and tree limbs that could not be washed out by our competitors. We even selected a skillful 3rd-grader to direct the operation! Through trial and error, we discovered the value of dense, heavy materials to withstand pressure and of spillways to divert water from our masterpiece of construction.

When the teacher came to the school doorway and rang the bell, ending the hour-long lunch recess, we triumphantly rolled down our wet pants and carried our shoes into the building. We eagerly anticipated and planned for the next day and the inescapable effort to reverse fortunes and build a dam upstream to wash out our competitors' creation. I wonder whether today's teachers would allow such intense play. Could the water possibly be polluted? What would parents say about the soiled clothing? Would the janitor complain about water and mud in the hallway? Would playing in mud be considered an intrusion on academic lessons? Could the school be sued if a child dropped a rock on his foot?

While driving through South Texas recently, I stopped at a small-town park to watch children play. They were in the act of changing the temporary amusement and thrills of merely sliding down a manufactured slide into a transcendental experience of belly-flopping into a mud hole. Having discovered a discarded bucket and pop bottle, they were carrying water from a hydrant and creating a large mud hole at the exit of the slide. As excitement grew they raced to the top of the slide, poured water on the slide to cool it from the 100-degree Texas heat (they were wearing cut-offs and shorts), and slid down by ones, twos, and threes, landing feet first, head first, tummy first in the mud below. Soon, their bodies were covered with mud, and their delight increased as they invented new ways of mastering the mud hole.

I asked the children if their parents knew they were playing in mud (many small-town children are still allowed to talk to strangers). They answered "no" with some signs of anxiety, but added, "We'll wash it off." When I left, they were using a garden hose to clean the mud from their bodies, still laughing and still relishing the great fun they were having. What children know and most adults have seemingly never learned is that every kid needs a few good

mud holes in his or her play life. When it comes to play value, and value for child development, mud holes are more than mere collections of water and dirt. They are heightened, transcendental experiences. Such experiences can be replicated in so many ways—some good for kids, some perhaps damaging.

Consider the above play scenarios and those of the kids in the neighborhood where I now live—a neighborhood populated largely by young upwardly mobile high tech workers. When I walk through the neighborhood with a former college dean and a former IBM trainer—all of us grandparents now—we observe and comment on the play lives of the children living there. The children arrive home on the school bus in late afternoon to deserted houses. They do not converse with us and look away if we speak to them. (You don't talk to strangers even though you have seen them in the neighborhood many times.) They go immediately inside, raid the refrigerator for junk food, and sit down for a long afternoon and sometimes evening of television, Internet play, or video games.

The children in my neighborhood don't play outside unless parents are home; thus, little or no outdoor play is possible until the weekend, which may be filled with lessons and organized activities. At the homeowner's association meeting, the parents occasionally talk about building a playground, but the property owners with no children do not want to share in the legal liability of maintaining one. There is a wonderful little park on the creek side adjacent to the neighborhood, but parents consider it too dangerous for children to go there alone.

Which of the above contexts is more likely to result in deep or transcendental play? One can observe children riveted to computer games for hours,

When playing out-of-doors, children naturally blend learning and fun.

with play senses elevated to a heightened state, clearly blotting out mental influences of the outside world. Yet they play mechanically—reacting to the demands of the machine—and often are engaging in extreme animated violence. The seemingly addicted mechanized game player may indeed engage in transcendental levels of play, but at what price? The games may make no demands for creativity, construction, socialization, or gross motor activity. The writers of the chapters to follow elaborate on the consequences of depriving children of traditional forms of outdoor play and substituting more passive entertainments.

Merely achieving the most heightened state of play in itself is not equivalent to coupling deep or transcendental play with natural, outdoor, free, and creative play contexts and materials. Growing numbers of contemporary children are losing contact with nature. Never having extensive experience in the woodlands or other wild places, they seemingly never bond with nature. Kids who grow up playing in and interacting with creeks, rivers, hills, valleys, trees, tree houses, private places in the bushes, special places, gardens, animals, and vacant lots reflect with passion about the joy derived from such experiences. Children with limited experience in nature reflect about the ticks, chiggers, mosquitoes, snakes, scorpions, and lack of modern conveniences (such as fast food venues). See the children's book *Roxaboxen* (McLerran, 1991) for a delightful, compelling look at transcendental play in a natural context. Lacking experience in coping with risks inherent in natural contexts, and deprived of playtime at school, they may never develop the intuition and physical skills to make themselves safe on modern playgrounds equipped with challenging, manufactured equipment.

With the development of national playground safety guidelines and standards during the 1980s and 1990s, American playgrounds were rapidly transformed from assortments of steel climbing, swinging, and sliding structures, installed on asphalt and concrete, to even broader choices of equipment, standardized to meet the new safety guidelines and standards. The national guidelines and standards quickly became the "national standard of care" for playground equipment, and litigation based on conformity to these standards blossomed. As consciousness of playground injuries and litigation heightened, manufacturers, designers, and sponsors of playgrounds became increasingly reluctant to act creatively, and a pattern of sameness in playground design quickly emerged. Only a few manufacturers sponsor research to assist them in designing new equipment and to provide a support base for their actions.

The litigious nature of American society has reached a level where parents are suing schools for injuries their children suffer from playing in playground nature areas or outdoor classroom habitats. One such case, active as this is being written, involves parents who are suing a university system for an injury allegedly suffered when their child fell on a stump in the forest area of a child development center playground. Despite the risk of being sued, a few professionals and organizations continue to work collaboratively with children and adults to preserve and create special, natural places for children's play.

The adventure playgrounds of Europe, especially those in Scandinavian countries, appear to be the most creative, exciting playgrounds in the world. European courts are less likely than their American counterparts to make large awards for playground injuries, and parents are less prone to sue. Despite exceptional challenges, the adventure playground injury record is reputed to be better than that of conventional playgrounds. Personal observations suggest that the intense activity of children leading to physical fitness and the skilled leadership of playleaders contribute to the positive safety record.

With respect to benefits for child development, there is good play, bad play, and no play. "Good play" is play that challenges children mentally, socially, and physically. It is creative and intense, fun and transcending; incorporates nature, raw materials, and loose parts; and engages children in traditional games. "Bad play" is overly mechanical, over-regulated, repetitious, violent, sadistic, and addictive. "No play," or play deprivation, results when misguided politicians and school systems eliminate recess and physical education for fear that they somehow interfere with academic achievement. "No play" also takes place when parents over-schedule lessons and events, and when their children's calendars simply cannot accommodate playtime or when parent's work schedules keep children indoors for extended periods.

Research is accumulating that demonstrates vividly the consequences of play deprivation in infants and young children (Frost, Wortham, & Reifel, 2005). For example, research on the consequences of play deprivation of Romanian orphans over extended periods indicates that the results can be equated with a common definition of child abuse—"Mental or emotional injury to a child that results in an observable and material impairment in the child's growth, development, or psychological functioning" (Texas Department of Protective and Regulatory Services, 1995, p. 10-1). When the conclusions from research on the consequences of play deprivation are compared to this definition, we reach an inescapable conclusion—deliberate deprivation of play is child abuse.

The plea here is not merely for play but for good play—play that promotes positive (not negative) social skills, physical skills, and cognitive skills, and that heals emotional injury. Contrary to prevailing views among a growing number of politicians and school boards, play promotes child development and equips children for academic tasks. In other words, play does not steal from reading, writing, and arithmetic, but rather enhances the social and cognitive bases for such skills. Play is a fundamental right of all children and must be preserved.

References

Ackerman, D. (1999). *Deep play*. New York: Random House.

Csikszentmihalyi, M. (1990). *Flow: The psychology of optimal experience*. New York: Harper & Row.

Frost, J. L., Wortham, S. C., & Reifel, S. (2005). *Play and child development* (2nd ed.). Columbus, OH: Merrill Prentice Hall.

Maslow, A. H. (1962). Some basic propositions of a growth and self-actualization psychology. In *Association for Supervision and Curriculum Development yearbook: Perceiving, behaving, becoming* (pp. 34-49). Washington, DC: Association for Supervision and Curriculum Development.

McLerran, A. (1991). *Roxaboxen*. New York: Lee & Shepard Books.

Texas Department of Protective and Regulatory Services. (1995). *Day-care center minimum standards and guidelines*. Austin, TX: Author.

Section I

The Out-of-Doors: History, Value, and Environment

CHAPTER 1

Outdoor Play Environments
A Look Back

Patricia A. Crawford

Patricia A. Crawford, Ph.D., is Associate Professor and Director of Undergraduate Studies in the College of Education, University of Central Florida, Orlando. She works with prospective and practicing teachers in the areas of early childhood, elementary, and language arts.

> *"Marian called it Roxaboxen . . .*
> *There across the road, it looked like any rocky hill—*
> *Nothing but sand and rocks, same old wooden boxes, cactus and*
> *greasewood and thorny ocotillo—*
> *But it was a special place."*
> —*Roxaboxen*, written by Alice McLerran and illustrated by Barbara Cooney, 1991

In *Roxaboxen*, a beautifully rendered children's book, the author-illustrator team documents the development of Roxaboxen, a little niche in the world that is at once simple and extraordinary; it is a "town" made from old boxes, amid resources found in the outdoor environment, and created and sustained by the energy, resourcefulness, and enthusiasm of children (Frost, Wortham, & Reifel, 2001). Based on a true story and presented as a personal memoir, *Roxaboxen* demonstrates the important and prominent role that outdoor explorations have played in the personal and collective socio-histories of children. Likewise, in *The Secret Garden* (Burnett, 1910/1997), two emotionally and physically burdened children find health and happiness as they discover the joy of play and socialization in a special, outdoor refuge. The author notes that as the garden was coming to life, the "two children were coming alive with it" (p. 283). Powerful in their own right, these stories drive home the point that children benefit from outdoor play in many ways, and that they need to have a special place in which to do it.

Changing Images of Outdoor Play Areas

Children have always enjoyed playing outdoors, and finding the type of play space that, at least for the moment, could be called their own and considered a space meant especially for them (Bilton, 1998; Brett, Moore, & Provenzo, 1993; Rivkin, 1995; Stine, 1997). Across time, these spaces have changed. Many educators have witnessed this evolution within their own lifetimes, having experienced the shift from sandlots and streets to purposefully planned asphalt cityscapes, to artistic and environmentally sensitive playgrounds, and even to the introduction of overt commercialization, in which many young children now identify the McDonald's Playplace as their playground of choice (Schlosser, 2002).

These changes are reflective of many factors, including: the evolving images and definition of childhood, new attention to standards of safety, conscious attention given to the purpose of playgrounds and other outdoor play and learning environments, and a cultural movement in which all things, including outdoor play, tend to be more regulated, structured, and controlled. In order to better understand the role of these areas designated for outdoor play in the current education world, it is necessary to look back to their historical roots and resulting evolution.

Past Perspectives on Play

Historically, adults have entertained a fickle relationship with both the concept of childhood and the nature of play. Ancient Greek and Egyptian cultures acknowledged childhood as a unique period of human development, and philosophers, dating back to Plato and Aristotle, considered play an important and influential element in children's lives (Frost, 1988; Hughes, 1999). Over time, however, these beliefs shifted markedly. By the height of the Renaissance, the distinctions between childhood and adulthood had been minimized. Children of this era often were sent to work at early ages and the significance of their play was devalued (Hughes, 1999).

Seventeenth- and 18th-century Europe gave birth to mixed views on these topics. Although child advocates such as Rousseau stressed the unique nature of childhood and the importance of nurturing children through play, many leading theologians and educators of the time discouraged play, viewing it as a frivolous waste of time that stood in stark contrast to the Protestant work ethic. Likewise, in the early days of America, the Puritans propagated the belief that play was a detriment to the extent to which it served as a distraction from work. Only after time did these beliefs give way to a broadened perspective of the nature of childhood and the role of play within it (Brett, Moore, & Provenzo, 1993; Frost, 1988; Hughes, 1999). With this socio-history, it is little wonder that the value of children's play typically has been marginalized and that the development of designated outdoor play spaces was not considered to be a priority until recent years.

Historical Roots of the American Playground

In contrast to the historical undervaluing of play, sports and outdoor games for older children and adults have been a part of American social life since colonial times. According to Albertson (1975), love for sports; a prevailing religious belief that physical activity could divert one from inappropriate, sinful behaviors; and recognition that such activities could have a

positive impact on one's health all contributed to advocacy for physical activities among youth. Eventually, these beliefs led to the inclusion of some formalized lessons related to physical activities, such as swimming, running, hiking, and a variety of games, in 19th-century schools. Most often, these activities were advocated only for older boys and conducted in "found" spaces (e.g., running took place in the surrounding countryside, swimming was taught in a nearby sound, etc.). Eventually, schools and communities would consider the need for designated outdoor play spaces and expand their attention to include the outdoor play needs of girls and younger children (Hendricks, 2001).

Information on the beginnings of formal playgrounds is somewhat vague and the history of the American playground is rather brief (Brett, Moore, & Provenzo, 1993; Frost & Klein, 1979; Hughes, 1999). Early influences on the development of formal playgrounds can be traced to early 19th-century Germany, when Gutsmuth introduced the concept of the outdoor gymnasium for the purpose of fitness and physical training (Frost & Wortham, 1988). When brought to the United States, these "gymnasia" consisted primarily of traditional indoor equipment placed outdoors, with the aim of increasing physical fitness among older boys. In general, the popularity of these gymnasia was rather short-lived (Frost, 1988; Frost & Wortham, 1988; Frost, Wortham, & Reifel, 2001).

Early attempts to support the outdoor play needs of young children were made in the late 19th century. Building on the theories of such noted educators as Rousseau, Pestalozzi, and Froebel, child advocates began to note the importance of play and the corresponding need to support such play in the lives of children. The first notable systematic attempt to provide designated outdoor play areas for young children in the United States involved the Boston sand gardens. These were large piles of sand designated for children's play, and were established in 1886 at the suggestion of Dr. Marie Zakrewska. Dr.

Zakrewska had visited Germany and based the idea on the sandpile playgrounds she saw in Berlin (Brett, Moore, & Provenzo, 1993; Frost & Wortham, 1988; Frost, Wortham, & Reifel, 2001).

Support for designated outdoor play areas was again garnered in 1887, with the passing of a New York City law that required the establishment of small parks and playgrounds throughout the city. During this time period, Jacob Riis, a journalist and reformer, noted the connection between the establishment of playgrounds and social improvement (Brett, Moore, & Provenzo, 1993). This work in the social science realm led to the beginnings of the American playground movement, in which playgrounds and outdoor play came to be valued for their potential impact on children's growth and development across the cognitive, moral, and social domains (Brett, Moore, & Provenzo, 1993).

While this social movement was taking place, support for quality playgrounds also was buoyed by those in the education community, championed by such noted leaders as Friedrich Froebel, Patty Smith Hill, Harriet Johnson, Lucy Sprague Mitchell, and Caroline Pratt. A look at education history demonstrates that the playground movement and the push to establish designated outdoor play areas took place in tandem with the nursery school and kindergarten movement (Frost & Wortham, 1988; Hartle & Johnson, 1993). Both of these movements emphasized the need for learning through exploration and free play and were a dramatic departure from traditional elementary schools of this era.

In the United States and abroad, adjacent outdoor play areas were both more readily available and more highly valued in nursery schools than in elementary programs. Elementary schools also tended to be much more structured than kindergartens or nursery schools, and their playgrounds developed (or in some cases, did not develop) accordingly (Bilton, 1998; Frost, Wortham, & Reifel, 2001). Bilton (1998) outlines a number of socio-historical influences that have contributed to the

difference between these two models of education and concludes that from a philosophical standpoint, "The pioneers of nursery education viewed childhood and people's lives in different ways from those who ran compulsory elementary education" (p. 17). Clearly, this difference in philosophy had a significant impact on the development and quality of playgrounds in both the early childhood and elementary arenas.

Eras in Playground Development

Joe L. Frost, a leading authority on outdoor play environments, has identified several distinct periods in the history of the American playground: the Manufactured Appliance Era, the Novelty Era, the Modular Design Era, and the Standardized Era. Playgrounds developed during each of these time periods were both reflective of, and contributed to, the prevailing social and educational frameworks of the period (Frost, 1987; Frost, 1992; Frost & Klein, 1979; Frost & Wortham, 1988; Frost, Wortham, & Reifel, 2001).

Frost designates the early part of the 20th century as the Manufactured Appliance Era. This era is noted for its push towards predictability and standardization; the standard playground prominently featured fixed apparatus such as slides, swings, and seesaws (Frost, 1988; Frost & Wortham, 1988; Frost, Wortham, & Reifel, 2001). Stine (1997) notes that, like many aspects of society in early 20th century America, playgrounds were influenced by a prevailing military model and mindset. This impact could be seen in the physical composition of the playground, which often had the appearance of a drill yard, complete with an asphalt base and enclosed with a chain-link fence. The impact of this model also was evident in the intended purposes of the playground, as places where children could "build character" (Stine, 1997).

The Manufactured Appliance Era contributed to the development of the "traditional" playground construct. However, it also contributed to a legacy of pain, thanks to a developmental mismatch between young children and the characteristic hulking equipment, dangerous heights, and hard surfaces, which resulted in an untold number of injuries. Sadly, the rugged steel and iron used in the construction of equipment during this era had an enduring quality that enabled these types of playgrounds to remain viable long after their inappropriate qualities were recognized. Thus, dangerous playgrounds and equipment still haunt us to a certain extent today, long after the development of safety standards that recommend against their use (Brett, Moore, & Provenzo, 1993; Hartle & Johnson, 1993).

The next era of playground development occurred during the post-World War II years of the 1950s and 1960s. This period was influenced by the factory model and industrial mindset that dominated American thought and work. As with their factory counterparts, schools placed a high value on hard work and high productivity. Outdoor play was viewed as a reward and a stress reliever from intensive school activities (Banta, 1993; Stine, 1997).

Part of what was dubbed the Novelty Era, playgrounds of this period were influenced by the work of architects, artists, and educators (Frost, Wortham, & Reifel, 2001). These playgrounds, which boasted novelty designs and concrete structures, were often thematic in nature, with structures and, in some cases, whole playgrounds developed around a single theme, such as airplanes, nautical life, or space exploration. These playgrounds, with their artistic structures and inviting themes, had a great deal of appeal and tended to have better safety records than the playgrounds built during the Manufactured Appliance Era. They were unsuccessful, however, to the extent that they failed to invite children to engage in higher levels of play and use the sculptures and equipment for a variety of purposes beyond the ones suggested by their architectural design (Brett, Moore, & Provenzo, 1993; Frost, Wortham, & Reifel, 2001; Hartle & Johnson, 1993).

The post-World War II era also ushered in the development of adventure playgrounds. These playgrounds, originally envisioned by Danish architect C. T. Sorenson, are continually evolving spaces that spring from a particular context and are designed to appeal to the natural interests of children. Activities such as building, digging, exploring nature, creating secret forts, gardening, and caring for animals are all possibilities on adventure playgrounds. Children on these playgrounds, under the supervision of qualified play leaders, are free to make significant choices regarding their play and other activities (Bengtsson, 1972; Frost, 1987; Frost, Wortham, & Reifel, 2001). These playgrounds require strong community participation and are known for being a bit "wilder" than other relatively tame and more regulated playgrounds (Brett, Moore, & Provenzo, 1993). Although these playgrounds were built on a child-centered model and enjoyed a considerable amount of popularity in Europe, their potential went relatively untapped in the United States, due to concerns about safety, the unkempt appearance of some adventure playgrounds, and a lack of qualified play leaders (Jalongo & Isenberg, 2001).

Playgrounds designed during the Modular Design Era (Frost, Wortham, & Reifel, 2001) of the 1970s and 1980s featured a variety of materials, with an increased emphasis on the use of wood and plastics. Many playgrounds included superstructures developed from modular units, which allowed for a wider range of designs and choices. As in other aspects of society, playground developers of this period placed an added emphasis on the importance of safety.

The period between the late 1980s and the present is known as the Standardized Era (Frost, Wortham, & Reifel, 2001). In this era, playground design is based on knowledge gained from the periods that have preceded it. As was the case in the Modular Design Era, today's playgrounds continue to feature modular equipment and superstructures that invite children to engage in many different types of activities at a variety of levels. In response to safety guidelines, playground equipment now tends to be made from nontoxic materials that are resistant to both heat and cold. Safety recommendations have been expanded to include other aspects of the environment, such as surface areas, terrain, and portable equipment. This has resulted in a renewed trend towards standardization, which has left playground developers with the challenge of balancing much-needed standards with the desires and unique needs of individual children, their communities, and the natural environment that surrounds them (Frost, Wortham, & Reifel, 2001; Hudson, Thompson, & Mack, 2000; Rivkin, 1995; Wardle, 1997).

Recontextualizing the Playground

Currently, we find ourselves witnessing a trend toward childhood obesity in ever-greater numbers due to lack of activity; toward children's alienation from the natural world as a result of urban and suburban lifestyles; and toward parents keeping their children indoors in the name of safety (Ebbeling, Pawlak, & Ludwig, 2002; Kupetz & Twiest, 2000; Rivkin, 1995; Schlosser, 2002; Sothern & Gordon, 2003; Stine, 1997; Sutterby & Frost, 2002). These factors are just some of the reasons why the development of playgrounds that are safe, developmentally appropriate, inclusive, environmentally sensitive, and engaging is a vital and significant task. Like early re-formers, current experts recognize that playgrounds are important places that offer the opportunity for play, social develop-ment, and a myriad of learning experiences. The playgrounds of today must be built upon a firm foundation of lessons learned from the past, as well as a strong forward vision for exemplary outdoor environments of the future.

References

Albertson, R. (1975). *Sports and games in New England schools and academies 1780-1860.* ERIC Document Reproduction Service No. 107598

Banta, M. (1993). *Taylored lives: Narrative productions in the age of Taylor, Veblen, and Ford.* Chicago: University of Chicago Press.

Bengtsson, A. (Ed.). (1972). *Adventure playgrounds.* New York: Praeger.

Bilton, H. (1998). *Outdoor play in the early years:*

Management and innovation. London: David Fulton Publishers.

Brett, A., Moore, R. C., & Provenzo, E. F. (1993). *The complete playground book.* Syracuse, NY: Syracuse University Press.

Burnett, F. H. (1997). *The secret garden.* New York: Scholastic. (Original work published 1910)

Ebbeling, C. B., Pawlak, D. B., & Ludwig, D. S. (2002). Childhood obesity: Public-health crisis, common sense cure. *Lancet, 360,* 473-482.

Frost, J. L. (1987, April). *Child development and playgrounds.* Paper presented at the National Convention of the American Alliance for Health, Physical Education, Recreation, and Dance. Las Vegas, NV. ED 281632.

Frost, J. L. (1988). Child development and playgrounds. In L. D. Bruya (Ed.), *Play spaces for children: A new beginning* (pp. 3-28). Reston, VA: American Alliance for Health, Physical Education, Recreation and Dance.

Frost, J. L. (1992). *Play and playscapes.* Albany, NY: Delmar.

Frost, J. L., & Klein, B. L. (1979). *Children's play and playgrounds.* Boston: Allyn & Bacon.

Frost, J. L., & Wortham, S. C. (1988). The evolution of American playgrounds. *Young Children, 43,* 19-28.

Frost, J. L., Wortham, S., & Reifel, S. (2001). *Play and child development.* Upper Saddle River, NJ: Prentice-Hall.

Hartle, L., & Johnson, J. E. (1993). Historical and contemporary influences of outdoor play environments. In C. H. Hart (Ed.), *Children on playgrounds: Research perspectives and applications* (pp. 14-42). Albany, NY: State University of New York Press.

Hendricks, B. E. (2001). *Designing for play.* Burlington, VT: Ashgate.

Hudson, S. D., Thompson, D., & Mack, M. G. (2000). Safe playgrounds: Increased challenges, reduced risks. *Dimensions of Early Childhood, 29,* 18-20.

Hughes, F. P. (1999). *Children, play, and development* (3rd ed.). Boston: Allyn & Bacon.

Jalongo, M. R., & Isenberg, J. P. (2001). *Creative expression and play in early childhood* (3rd ed.). Upper Saddle River, NJ: Prentice-Hall.

Kupetz, B. N., & Twiest, M. M. (2000). Nature, literature and young children: A natural combination. *Young Children, 55*(1), 59-63.

McLerran, A. (1991). *Roxaboxen.* Illustrated by B. Cooney. New York: Scholastic.

Rivkin, M. S. (1995). *The great outdoors: Restoring children's right to play outside.* Washington, DC: National Association for the Education of Young Children.

Schlosser, E. (2002). *Fast food nation: The dark side of the all-American meal.* New York: HarperCollins.

Sothern, M., & Gordon, S. (2003). Prevention of obesity in young children: A critical challenge for medical professionals. *Clinical Pediatrics, 42,* 101-111.

Stine, S. (1997). *Landscapes for learning: Creating outdoor environments for children and youth.* New York: John Wiley & Sons.

Sutterby, J. A., & Frost, J. L. (2002). Making playgrounds fit for children and children fit on playgrounds. *Young Children, 57*(3), 36-41.

Wardle, F. (1997). Playgrounds: Questions to consider when selecting equipment. *Dimensions of Early Childhood, 25,* 9-15.

CHAPTER 2

Playscapes
Rural, Urban, and Suburban

Rey A. Gomez

Rey A. Gomez is an Associate Professor and Director of the Initial Teacher Certification Program for Early Childhood Education at Arizona State University, Tempe.

lay is a many-splendored thing! It allows children the opportunity to be themselves, challenges them to be creative and spontaneous, gives them the tools for becoming critical thinkers and problem solvers, provides risk-taking behaviors, and helps them construct meaning for the world around them. It enables children to promote a healthy image of self as they view the perspectives of others in socio-dramatic play, and it enables them to become explorers and scientists as they manipulate objects and predict changes.

Play gives children the opportunity to develop positive relationships with family members, with other adults, and with other children. A child's imagination is engaged and enhanced through play activities, and is a powerful means of establishing dreams and aspirations for the future. What better venue do children have in which to pursue this development than the outdoor play setting?

This chapter examines outdoor play settings for children ages 8 through 12 years, with an emphasis on the urban/public, suburban, and rural settings. Recommendations for organizing and implementing quality play environments that are challenging and engaging for children and their families are provided, and the role of advocacy in developing these play environments through the cooperation of school districts and local, city, and state governments is explored.

Outdoor Play

Outdoor play offers children many benefits and unique opportunities to develop their physical, cognitive, communicative, and social skills. As Rivkin (1995) explains, young children playing outdoors often experience a sense of freedom that encourages them to become involved in interactive games that foster language and create authentic opportunities for problem solving. Flynn and Kieff (2002) describe how a child's motor development and manipulative skills are enhanced by the spaciousness of outdoor areas and the availability of large equipment for climbing and sliding. Older children in the elementary grades also gain from these activities.

Outdoor play allows children the flexibility to play and interact with the environment and with others. Additionally, the outdoor environment enables children to experience all of the wonders of nature through the use of such natural play materials as sand, water, grass, trees, living things, and other people. Very simply stated, outdoor play enhances a child's development and allows for positive interactions with other children and adults. As Talbot and Frost (1989) state,

We can create with children playscapes that are fitting for the magical child if we feel it is important enough. But we must be willing to transcend the traditional and the scholarly and engage once again in the mystical, the enchanting and the elusive. (p. 12)

Outdoor play enables children to engage in different physical activities, particularly gross-motor activities, such as running, jumping, and climbing. Johnson, Christie, and Yawkey (1999) note, "Outdoor play provides opportunities for children to engage in gross motor activities needed for proper physical development. In addition, outdoor play appears to facilitate pretend play in middle-class boys and in low-income children of both genders" (p. 259).

It often has been stated that outdoor play is no longer as valued as it was during the periods of the Froebel kindergartens, Progressivism, and early nursery schools. According to Wellhousen (2002), "Today, the basic need to play outdoors is largely overlooked and the multitude of opportunities to learn from the outdoors is underestimated in most early childhood programs serving children from infancy through third grade" (p. 2). Therefore, the need exists to examine the outdoor environment to ensure that children, elementary-age children in particular, can benefit from a rich and challenging outdoor play setting.

Children need safe, appropriate, and well-planned outdoor environments in which to explore ideas and concepts, develop an appreciation of nature, exercise their bodies, and form social ties (Rivkin, 1995). Rivkin goes on to decry the loss of access to natural areas, as children today seem to know less about nature and have greater difficulty in establishing empathy for the environment. In light of this, the following are proposed to restore safe and creative outdoor play environments: greenways that serve as corridors of protected open space that connects parks and playgrounds; urban initiatives that include revitalizing projects to make cities safer and better places to live and play; child-aware land developments, which are planned communities that set aside areas for children to play; and efforts to reduce traffic and make streets safer for play (Rivkin, 1995).

Over-scheduling and lack of play and outdoor activity in children's lives are concerns. Recently, hundreds of professors, recreation workers, playground designers, and play advocates from more than 40 countries met at Hofstra University for a conference on children's right to play. In addition, parent groups are advocating for more recess time at elementary schools, to offset the pressures from school officials looking to extend the school day and encouraging the highest level of academics at the lowest possible age. Many play advocates have stated that some of this structured learning is counterproductive.

Urban Playgrounds

Prior to the 20th century, most outdoor play occurred in unstructured neighborhood or rural settings. Between 1880 and 1920, however, a concerted effort focused on establishing a network of playgrounds. This playground movement resulted in part from the concern about the effects of the Industrial Revolution and the growing numbers of impoverished immigrant children who had no place to play, except on city streets (Brett, Moore, & Provenzo, 1993; Mergen, 1982). At this time, city leaders believed poor children would be much better off playing in organized settings.

The result of this concern was the construction of the traditional playground, with its emphasis on exercise through the use of swings, jungle gyms, slides, and other immovable equipment, all set in concrete and asphalt. According to Frost and Jacobs (1995), most of those "traditional" playgrounds in public parks, public schools, and child care centers are hazardous and ill-equipped.

Play in urban outdoor settings is quite restrictive, due to the lack of space for children to play. Many of the current play settings are the traditional ones that emphasize exercise and gross motor skills. Rising crime rates and parents' sense of insecurity about leaving children unattended restrict children's freedom to play in their own neighborhoods. Furthermore, many schools, in response to the pressure for academic excellence, have shortened or eliminated recess altogether. Children's and families' hectic schedules also limit outdoor play.

Frost and Jacobs (1995) report that urban children's activities are often restricted by the scarcity of other children, the lack of toys, and unsafe or age-inappropriate playground equipment. A movement to re-design and re-equip playgrounds has been growing due to dissatisfaction with available traditional playgrounds. Also influential in this trend is a backlash against the cognitive emphasis in early childhood, the success of European play environments, an increasing awareness of deficiencies in traditional American playgrounds, and the accumulation of experience with new types of playgrounds (Frost, 1978). Additionally, many childhood professionals have recognized the significant value that outdoor environments have for enhancing children's cognitive, social, emotional, and physical development.

Recent innovative playground design replaces cold iron and steel with wood, powder-coated metal, and plastic (Hartle & Johnson, 1993). Surfaces such as sand, wood chips, and rubber have replaced concrete and asphalt. Also, current playgrounds feature loose items, such as sand and water. While suburban play environments often include the neighborhood park and adjacent areas that offer exposure to nature and real-life materials, the urban playscape may not.

Wardle (1995) emphasizes the need for urban schools to provide field trips to botanical gardens, river embankments, and outdoor environments, all of which allow children to explore nature. Other possible field trip locations are forests, wetlands, a working farm, a working dairy, old quarries, and perhaps even a ranch.

Public school playgrounds are similar to those of public parks, as most are outfitted with antiquated, developmentally inappropriate, hazardous equipment and they receive little or no maintenance.

In order for playgrounds to meet the broad play needs of children, there must be physical climbing equipment, equipment and materials for dramatic play, constructional play and organized games, and special provisions for natural elements such as water, sand, and living things. The best playgrounds have places for digging, playing in water, constructing, gardening, attracting animals and private and group socialization areas. (Frost & Jacobs, 1995, p. 16)

Contemporary Urban Play Areas

Today's emphasis on technology and computers appears to leave little time for children to play outdoors. Children no longer have the freedom to play when and where they choose. Their lives are controlled by the unforgiving schedules of adults and frequently by their own relentless schedules, both in and out of school, from daylight to dark (Frost & Jacobs, 1995).

A Right To Play movement across the United States is making the case that children need more time and space to be children. This growing recognition of children's need for play in outdoor urban areas has led children's museums and a growing number of adventure playgrounds to offer infinitely better opportunities for free and pure play. As an example, the Family Museum currently being developed in Phoenix, Arizona, represents a unique facility where families and children can play and learn together. The Family Museum recently acquired a city bus, donated by the city of Phoenix, that volunteers, play advocates, and professional personnel transformed into a play environment filled with challenging and exciting play activities. The bus serves as a mobile museum that travels to various areas in the city, enabling children and families to experience creative play activities. As there is often a lack of space to play in large urban areas, this is an innovative example of creating new play opportunities for children.

In urban areas, a growing number of park and school playgrounds are being designed to accommodate both the social and physical play needs of children. One such playground is the adventure playground, which was first developed in Scandinavia decades ago. These types of playgrounds contain construction zones for building materials and tools, water and sand areas, digging areas, fire pits for cooking, climbing structures, cable rides, organized games areas, garden and garden tools, nature areas, and a range of animals, from rabbits to horses (Frost & Jacobs, 1995).

One of the key components of adventure playgrounds is a well-trained play leader. This individual facilitates all of the different types of play possible on an adventure playground. A unique feature is the maximum freedom allowed to children for their play. According to Frost and Jacobs (1995), adventure playgrounds are making a difference in the lives of children, while promoting skill development and emotional stability and a reduction in juvenile delinquency. This type of playground centers on the interests of children while promoting creativity, risk-taking behaviors, and critical thinking skills.

Other types of playgrounds found in urban areas are the so-called "cookie cutter" playgrounds. These playgrounds are complex, and contain fixed equipment that serve multiple functions. Some of these playgrounds consist of a superstructure, supplemented with sand and water play, storage facilities, dramatic play structures, gardens, pet facilities, and nature areas; areas that accommodate all children, including those with disabilities, are also available. These contemporary playgrounds are still considered to be of a higher quality than the traditional playground.

Suburban/Community Playgrounds

As for the nature of residential, community, or suburban playgrounds, a new movement among various communities is paving the way for more creative and safe play environments for children. These new types of playgrounds are being developed with the assistance of nonprofit organizations and community volunteers. Community playgrounds are essential, as many families often do not have the space or the equipment to maintain a developmentally appropriate and challenging playspace at home. Therefore, a need exists to develop creative and challenging outdoor environments for children in residential areas.

An example of how this can be done is found in the work of Leather and Associates, an architectural design firm with many years' experience in designing community playgrounds. The first question they ask families and children is what should be included in the new playground. They incorporate the ideas presented by the families and children into the design of the playground. Committees are formed for each phase of the project, including fundraising, purchasing or obtaining donated materials, community outreach, providing meals during the work week, and gathering volunteers (Wellhousen, 2002). Community volunteers donate their time, labor, and expertise in helping to construct the new outdoor setting.

Other communities choose to develop their playgrounds through a barn-raising approach, or they opt to buy manufactured equipment. With a volunteer labor force (Wellhousen, 2002) to plan, design, and build the playground, a sense of community pride can be achieved while reducing costs. Individuals who wish to pursue this type of approach can secure the services of KaBOOM! (2000), a national nonprofit organization, created to assist communities in building playgrounds. KaBOOM! provides basic information on building safe age-appropriate environments, provides extensive advice on completing a community-built playground, offers publications and resources, and hosts a database that matches funding, in-kind, and or human resource support from corporate sponsors. The key is securing a strong commitment from the community to build and maintain these playgrounds.

Rural Settings

Outdoor environments in rural areas are perhaps the most natural settings in which children can play, offering the opportunity to explore and appreciate nature. These environments hold an abundance of rich and authentic materials that children can use in their play, such as trees to climb, ponds of water on which to sail small boats, and sand and mud to form. Wide spaces offer the freedom to engage in imaginative and creative play. Talbot and Frost (1989) suggest that an increase in greenery of any kind, including gardens, woods, groves, and orchards, will help to increase imagination and creativity, or what they call "mystical thinking" and "enchanting experiences," in outdoor playscapes.

Planning Outdoor Environments

The outdoor play environment should offer ample opportunities to interact safely with the elements of nature. Creating a garden is a good example of learning how to balance the elements to create life (Talbot, 1985), and children can watch seeds transform into plants. Outdoor environments should allow sand and water play, and digging for exploration. Other recommended components include a fireplace for cooking and a treehouse for imaginative play. An essential element of all outdoor play environments is children's safety, and adults should provide careful supervision and spend time playing with children in these environments.

Johnson, Christie, and Yawkey (1999) have suggested certain criteria for planning optimal outdoor play environments, which they developed from a series of articles by Wardle (1988, 1990, 1997). They address surfaces, areas and equipment, materials, safety, and adaptations for children with special needs. The authors suggest that playgrounds should have different surfaces for promoting different kinds of play, while ensuring safety. Flat, grassy, and dirt areas allow for quick-moving activities and gross motor skills. Hard surfaces are suggested for bikes and wagons. Soft and absorbent surfaces, such as sand, pea gravel, or wood chips, should be placed under all equipment for safety reasons.

Playgrounds should contain a variety of equipment to promote a wide range of play behaviors. Structures for climbing and balancing, equipment for grabbing, areas for crawling and digging, and equipment for jumping are a few suggestions. Equipment such as rope and tire nets, ladders, balance beams, swing chains, and tools for playing in the sand also are beneficial. The outdoor play environment should promote social play, dramatic play, constructional play, and games with rules. The environment should include an area that is conducive for building and constructing all types of objects.

The playground also should be accessible for all children, including children with special needs. Johnson, Christie, and Yawkey (1999) suggest that all playgrounds should have wide gates and pathways, plus cuts in curbs, to provide access for those children in wheelchairs. They also recommend lining the pathways with Braille markers for visually impaired children and adapting basic equipment with additional railings for support. It is critical to ensure that the adaptations for children with disabilities do not pose safety hazards for the other children.

Recommendations for ensuring a safe, engaging, and challenging outdoor play setting include the following:

- Allow plenty of time for children to play outdoors
- Develop a routine/schedule that allows for outdoor play
- Allow yourself the opportunity to play with children, if invited
- Keep a watchful eye on children to ensure safety
- Install creative and challenging equipment so that children can maximize and enjoy the outdoor environment
- Develop an advocacy group within your neighborhood that supports outdoor play environments
- Work with the local school district and local government to ensure quality outdoor play environments for children.

Within the home setting, the outdoor yard can be transformed into a play environment for children through the use of practical materials that children should have access to and even can help develop. These can include a garden area for growing flowers or vegetables; a large, open space for gross motor play; real materials, such as sand, water, and mud; constructional materials, such as lumber, for building; mobile equipment, such as large wagons and bikes; play crates or prop boxes, such as containers for loose parts; areas where children can paint; a fire pit for cooking; climbing equipment; hiking and biking paths; a shaded area; an area for dramatic play; digging areas; and opportunities for running, climbing, and chasing.

Summary

Given the fast-paced world that we all live in and the stress that children feel to compete and achieve academic success, the need for quality, challenging, and creative outdoor play environments could not be greater. Many of us have wonderful memories of playing outdoors: climbing trees; playing with sand, water, and mud; playing with a water hose; utilizing our imaginations while swinging on a swing (i.e., pretending to be a trapeze artist); planting a vegetable garden; roasting marshmallows over an open fire pit; building a treehouse; and running through a large grassy area. While on these pursuits, we forgot all our troubles. A vast amount of research supports play in outdoor settings as a key contributor to a child's cognitive, social, emotional, and physical development. Whether children are playing in a city park, a suburban park, an adventure playground, or on a large farm, playing outdoors provides a sense of joy as they explore, learn, and dream.

References

Brett, A., Moore, R., & Provenzo, E. (1993). *The complete playground book.* Syracuse, NY: Syracuse University Press.

Flynn, L. L., & Kieff, J. (2002). Including everyone in outdoor play. *Young Children, 57*(3), 20-26.

Frost, J. (1978). The American playground movement. *Childhood Education, 54,* 176-182.

Frost, J., & Jacobs, P. J. (1995). Play deprivation: A factor in juvenile violence. *Dimensions of Early Childhood, 23*(3), 14-20.

Hartle, L., & Johnson, J. (1993). Historical and contemporary influences of outdoor play environments. In C. Hart (Ed.), *Children on playgrounds: Research perspectives and applications* (pp. 14-42). Albany, NY: State University of New York Press.

Johnson, J. E., Christie, J. F., & Yawkey, T. D. (1999). *Play and early childhood development.* New York: Longman.

KaBOOM! (2000). *Getting started kit.* Washington, DC: KaBOOM!

Mergen, B. (1982). *Play and playthings: A reference guide.* Westport, CT: Greenwood Press.

Rivkin, M. (1995). *The great outdoors: Restoring children's right to play outside.* Washington, DC: National Association for the Education of Young Children.

Talbot, J. (1985). Plants in children's outdoor environments. In J. L. Frost & S. Sunderlin (Eds.), *When children play* (pp. 243-251). Olney, MD: Association for Childhood Education International.

Talbot, J., & Frost, J. L. (1989). Magical playscapes. *Childhood Education, 66,* 11-19.

Wardle, F. (1988). Is your playground physically fit? *Scholastic Pre-K Today, 27*(7), 21-26.

Wardle, F. (1990). Are we taking the fun out of playgrounds? *Daycare and Early Education, 18*(1), 30-34.

Wardle, F. (1995). Bruderhof education: Outdoor school. *Young Children, 50*(3), 68-73.

Wardle, F. (1997). Outdoor play: Designing, building and remodeling playgrounds for young children. *Early Childhood News, 9*(2), 36-42.

Wellhousen, K. (2002). *Outdoor play every day: Innovative play concepts for early childhood.* Albany, NY: Delmar.

CHAPTER 3

Including Students With Special Needs in Outdoor Play

Judith Kieff and Linda Flynn

Judith Kieff, Ed.D., is an Associate Professor in the Department of Curriculum and Instruction at the University of New Orleans. Linda Flynn, Ph.D., is an Associate Professor in the Department of Special Education at the University of New Orleans.

All elementary school students, regardless of their developmental differences, have multiple opportunities to learn and develop when engaged in outdoor play and learning activities. In inclusive settings, students with disabilities are considered fully participating members of the group and take meaningful roles in class activities. Outdoor play is an important aspect of inclusive elementary schools because it provides sensory-rich opportunities that allow all students to explore their physical environment while interacting with children of differing abilities. The play of students with special needs is richer and more sophisticated when they have opportunities to play with peers who are typically developing (Esposito & Koorland, 1989; Kohl & Beckman, 1984). Similarly, students who are developing in more typical ways gain an appreciation for individual differences and develop respect for others' contributions when they engage in inclusive play activities (Biklin, 1992; Stainback & Stainback, 1990). As Covert (1995) explains, all of society benefits when children are able to work through their biases and fears regarding differences among people.

However, the mere presence of children with special needs or differing ability levels in inclusive outdoor settings will not automatically result in the kinds of play and learning activities that support the development of cognitive and social skills, empathy, and tolerance (Bergen, 1993; Esposito & Koorland, 1989; Jenkins, Odom, & Speltz, 1989; Kohl & Beckman, 1984; Lamorey & Bricker, 1993; Pickett, Griffith, & Rogers-Adkinson, 1993), because there are often fundamental differences between the play behaviors of students with special needs and those of their typically developing peers. Pugmire-Stoy (1992) states that many students who are developing in typical ways often spontaneously engage in play activities, consistently seek new challenges as they play, recognize a need for assistance, and readily ask for it. However, students with special needs may lack concentration skills and the drive to initiate and sustain play for an extended period of time, or may process information more slowly than typically developing peers (Li, 1985). They also may lack the ability to challenge themselves through play, or the means of asking for assistance when needed (Buchanan & Cooney, 2000; Hughes, 1999). These difficulties are particularly significant during outdoor activities, because of the multiple distractions inherent in this environment. Due to these characteristics, a student with special needs may tend to isolate himself from other children during outside play.

Preventing tendencies towards isolation is particularly crucial during middle childhood, when the peer group becomes a meaningful source of emotional support. During these years, the development of friendships and acceptance by one's peers is of prime importance to the development of self-esteem (Hughes, 1999). In a review of research, Pavri (2001) states: "Children with disabilities, particularly children with learning disabilities and mental retardation, are more vulnerable to feelings of loneliness than their peers without disabilities" (p. 53). Two factors contribute to this feeling of loneliness. First, students with disabilities may have difficulty reading and processing social cues and developing social relationships

(Haager & Vaughn, 1995); second, educators may inadvertently limit the opportunities for students with disabilities to fully engage in the kind of activities that foster the development of supportive friendships with a heterogeneous group of peers (Pavri, 2001). Outdoor play offers a rich opportunity for all students to engage in collaborative activities that foster a sense of acceptance and belonging and lead to the formation of friendships. In order to develop the full potential of outdoor play, however, teachers must carefully design both the social and physical environments and choose activities and strategies that promote optimal interaction for all children.

Planning for Inclusive Outdoor Play

Students with special needs often encounter unique obstacles to outside play; therefore, they may require environmental and social supports, in the form of adaptations of existing playground spaces and equipment or modifications of teaching and intervention strategies, to facilitate involvement in outdoor activities. Adaptations or modifications enable students to participate in activities at the highest possible level and therefore receive maximum benefit from their experience. These supports should be designed to: 1) facilitate the entry of students with special needs into activities, and 2) allow them to sustain their involvement, thereby taking optimal advantage of the outside learning environment and interaction with peers. The following principles, adapted from Erwin and Schreiber (1999), suggest guidelines to consider when designing supports that foster inclusion.

Supports should:

- Be as non-stigmatizing and unobtrusive as possible
- Reflect students' rights to exercise control over the environment, make choices for themselves, and maintain independence
- Be developed with input from family members
- Be monitored and evaluated consis-

tently to ensure effectiveness
- Be provided by peers (when feasible and safe to do so)
- Be presented in an accepting climate that promotes membership in the learning community.

Teachers will need to gather specific information about the interests, skills, likes, dislikes, challenges, and abilities of a student with special needs when designing supports and planning for safe and effective outdoor environments and activities.

This information about a student's needs and abilities should represent a broad range of perspectives related to the student's special circumstances. An interdisciplinary team of individuals familiar with the child and the existing outdoor environment should compile observations and data. This team could include some, but not necessarily all, of the following individuals: family members, speech and language therapist, physical and occupational therapist, physical education teacher, classroom teacher, school nurse, program administrator, and the child. Whether the team consists of two members or five, it is imperative that the strengths and needs of the student are carefully considered when designing adaptations that will foster the student's participation in outdoor activities. This discussion could become a vital part of the student's Individual Education Plan (IEP). The following talking points (adapted from Flynn & Kieff, 2002) are designed to facilitate team discussions related to achieving a child's optimal involvement in outdoor activities.

- What are the student's current abilities related to movement, cognition, communication, and social interaction?
- What components of the outdoor environment are particularly pleasing or interesting to the student?
- What barriers currently exist that impede the student's access to materials, equipment, and peers?
- What motivates the student to explore his environment and interact with others?

- Which peers in the class have similar interests and therefore could be included in activity groups?
- What tends to overstimulate or even frighten the student?
- What are the current goals for the student regarding cognitive, physical, social-emotional, and communicative development?
- What opportunities does the existing playground, and routines related to playground use, offer for the development of these current goals?
- What easy or inexpensive changes should be made to materials, equipment, or playground routines to enhance the opportunities for the student to fulfill identified goals, interact with peers, and have fun?
- What extensive or complex changes should be made to materials, equipment, or routines to enhance opportunities for the student to fulfill identified goals, interact with peers, and have fun?

Information gathered from these interdisciplinary team discussions can be used to foster a greater understanding of how to best utilize outdoor space, equipment, and materials to benefit the child's overall physical, cognitive, communication, and emotional development.

Modifying the Outdoor Environment

A first step in modifying outdoor environments and activities to include all students is to reflect on the amount of multisensory activities available outdoors. Multisensory experiences include those activities that utilize the senses of touch, smell, sight, taste, and hearing, and that incorporate movement. A student who has compromised sensory input (such as blindness, deafness, or physical limitations) may not be able to use all of the senses available to typically developing peers; she will need help to use those senses available to her to understand and explore the outside environment. For example, teachers might think games of catch would not be appro-

priate activities for a student who is blind or has low vision. By using an adapted ball (e.g., one that is equipped with a sounding device), however, the student with low vision can successfully participate.

Teachers should survey the existing play yard and categorize typical play activities according to the major sense modality used. This process will clarify the types of adaptations that might need to be made or activities that may need to be added to the outdoor repertoire to increase the likelihood that all students will find activities they can participate in comfortably.

Adding a garden to the outdoor environment will provide a rich multisensory experience for all. Bringing art and music activities outdoors also will increase the multisensory nature of the play yard, as will adding a workbench or bringing construction materials outside. Developing an activity area with tables and chairs will foster engagement in board games, collaborative reading and writing activities, and science investigations. Multisensory activities are mandatory for students with certain disabilities, but also will facilitate learning for all students.

Linking Supports That Foster Inclusion

Students with special needs may require a series of environmental and social supports that are linked together to promote opportunities for successful involvement in outdoor activities. For example, installing an environmental support, such as a ramp, may allow a student in a wheelchair to enter an elevated area of the play yard, but the student may need additional social supports to enter the ongoing play of peers. It is important to remember that students with the same diagnosis or disability, such as loss of sight, may have similar characteristics, but each student will differ regarding individual strengths and need for assistance and will require unique supports. Examples, adapted from Flynn and Kieff (2002), of possible environmental and social supports that would facilitate interactions among elementary school children are described next.

The Student Who Is Blind or Has Low Vision

Environmental Supports (adaptations of equipment or space):

- Note the audible cues that are associated with particular areas of the play yard. For example, on the blacktop area, the sounds of bouncing balls or children jumping ropes serve as identifying markers for play activities. In the field, students can be heard playing softball or soccer. Other areas or boundaries may not be so easily identified. These locations should be marked with audible cues, such as wind chimes or bells. Cones with audible devices are available and make excellent boundary markers.
- Create and enforce playground rules that ensure unattended equipment will not block walking spaces between play activities. Make someone responsible each play period to check pathways to ensure that potential hazards are removed.
- Provide outdoor equipment and play activities that utilize the senses of hearing, touch, and smell, as well as movement, and that encourage interaction with others. Materials that promote exploration through touch are those with interesting, diverse textures, such as Koosh balls and bumpy balls. Smells can be incorporated into outdoor art activities by adding scented extracts to the paint. Movement can be experienced through the addition of adaptive swings, jump ropes, and parachute games.

Social Supports (modifications of teaching or intervention strategies):

- Orient the student to the major features of the outdoor area: walkways, climbing structures, garden, and team play areas. Take a tour of the playground and include another child who can offer her arm/elbow to guide the child who is blind.
- Use the student's name when verbally directing activities, as he will not be able to see physical gestures such as pointing or gesturing.
- When the student enters the playground, help her identify the voices of classmates so she will know which children are playing on the climbing structures, playing with a ball, or working in the gardening area. Provide the child only as much assistance as necessary to join ongoing activities.

The Student Who Is Deaf or Has a Hearing Loss

Environmental Supports (adaptations of equipment or space):

- Create visual signals, such as signs, color signals, flags, or flashing lights, and pair them with traditional verbal signals such as whistles or bells.
- Make sure the student can see most areas of the playground from any given spot, because much of the student's information about his environment is visual. Remove extraneous walls, fences, or hedges that might block his view of peers playing and thereby prevent him from joining in.
- Provide outdoor equipment and activities that utilize other senses available to the student, including touch, smell, and movement. Examples of activities that are enjoyable for all include dodge ball, tether ball, bouncing and catching balls or Frisbees, shooting baskets, jump rope games, and such movement games as flying kites, parachute games, hopscotch, Simon Says, and Mother May I.

Social Supports (modifications of teaching or intervention strategies):

- Obtain the student's attention through touch or gestures before giving directions.
- Make sure the student can see your lips, with no shadows blocking your face, when giving directions.
- Be sure the student who is deaf and his peers are positioned so they can easily see each other's faces and gestures.
- Pair gestures, prompts, and visual cues with verbal instructions to communicate information. Gestures

may include pointing and sign language. Prompts may include physical assistance. Visual cues may include the utilization of concrete materials and modeling.

- If sign language is the mode of communication, learn basic signs and teach them to classmates.

The Student Who Has Physical Challenges

Environmental Supports (adaptations of equipment or space):

- Furnish specifically adapted play and recreation equipment when necessary. This might include modified swings, prone standers, and tables that promote both independent and interactive participation in such games as jacks, marbles, and art activities.
- Increase the width of balance beams and modify slippery surfaces.
- Use soft balls, such as Nerf or cloth balls, or other lightweight objects to facilitate throwing and catching when a student lacks strength and endurance.
- Use enlarged balls, such as beach balls, and other large objects to make catching easier for the student who is unable to grasp smaller objects.

Social Supports (modifications of teaching or intervention strategies):

- Position the student with physical challenges so that she can achieve the maximum range of motion, muscle control, and visual contact with materials and other children. For example, a student may need to lie on her side or use a bolster to access materials and interact with others during play.
- Encourage playground activities that a student with limited use of his hands or upper body can do with his lower body and feet. Examples include foot painting, group jump rope games, tag, dance, dramatic play, and games that focus on kicking a ball.
- Encourage playground activities that a student with limited use of his legs, feet, and lower body can do independently and successfully with his upper body. Ex-

amples include building projects, art activities, card and board games, marbles, jacks, collaborative reading and drama activities, and gardening.

The Student Who Has an Autism Spectrum Disorder

Environmental Supports (adaptations of equipment or space):

- Moderate the amount of time a student spends on the playground to fit the individual's ability to adjust successfully, and prevent the student from becoming overstimulated.
- Include pets in the outside area. Some students may interact with pets before they will interact with people. Allow the student to touch the animal and participate in feeding and other care activities, such as cleaning habitats.
- Organize sections of the playground in ways that provide physical boundaries for the student. Use cones or existing play materials, such as tunnels, barrels, or large cardboard boxes made into play structures.

Social Supports (modifications of teaching or intervention strategies):

- Maintain awareness of the kinds of situations and events that may trigger fear or overstimulation, in order to prevent undesired behaviors. Such events may include inconsistent or unstructured environments, new situations, illness, or fatigue.
- Limit the outside rules, communicate them clearly and in multiple ways, and enforce then firmly, kindly, and consistently.
- Provide structured activities that are relatively free from distractions for students who have difficulty paying attention or controlling their movements.
- Provide extra support when teaching new games or activities. Break instruction into simple, sequential steps and reinforce the student's efforts appropriately.
- Increase predictability and consistency in outside routines. Prepare the

student for what comes next through verbal and concrete prompts. For example, put a ball in a student's hand to indicate it is time to go outside while simultaneously using words to describe the event.

- Include repetition and modeling when giving directions to a student with perceptual and/or sensory input disabilities.
- Make sure that a student is aware of physical changes to the playground prior to experiencing the change. For example, if a new structure is added to an existing climbing apparatus, tell the student before he goes to the playground. Show him a picture of the new structure and describe how it could be used. Accompany him to the area and support his interaction with the equipment and with others as they experiment with the addition.

The Student Who Has Cognitive Delays

Environmental Supports (adaptations of equipment or space):

- Reduce the number of choices a student has regarding play activities to a manageable level.
- Vary the difficulty of an activity so that the student can be successful. For example, modify an obstacle course to encourage independent, successful completion.
- Include noncompetitive games and activities so that all students can feel successful and enjoy individual achievements.

Social Supports (modifications of teaching or intervention strategies):

- Keep the vocabulary and sentence structure within the student's level of understanding when explaining situations and teaching new games and skills.
- Remind the student of various types of play activities available and provide her support when making choices.
- Use repetition and examples to explain an idea.

A simple list of suggested environmental and social supports for students with specific disabilities, like the one presented here, is a place to start, but will not provide teachers with enough information to create the best combination of supports to enable a particular student to utilize the outdoor learning environment effectively. It is important that teachers, family members, and specialists work as an interdisciplinary team to design the specific supports necessary for each student to become fully engaged in inclusive outdoor play.

Creating a Culture of Inclusion on the Playground

Creating appropriate supports that allow a student with special needs to fully utilize the outdoor environment is an important step toward establishing inclusive outdoor activities. An equally important component is the development of a peer culture among classmates that recognizes both the strengths and challenges that face all students, and is accepting of the differences among students. The creation of this culture begins in the classroom as children get to know each other. Teachers, therapists, and family members can help classmates understand the nature of a particular disability by providing information and encouraging questions. Elementary school students with disabilities may be able to share their own stories, strengths, challenges, and wishes for play activities with their classmates. Many children's literature selections and videos will help students understand and empathize with the challenges that children with special needs face on a daily basis. As students learn more about each other, they have clearer ideas about how to interact with each other effectively. This knowledge will increase the likelihood of interactive play and decrease the incidence of isolation and loneliness among students with special needs.

The development of an accepting classroom climate that nurtures a sense of belonging, membership, trust, and mutual respect can be extended to the outdoor environment. Margalit (1994) identified several strategies teachers could use to encourage a climate of acceptance: 1) reduce conflict by fostering friendships between classmates; 2) place emphasis on individual growth; 3) reduce competition in the classroom (and subsequently, outdoor activities); and 4) establish clear expectations among students regarding their supportive interactions. Pavri and Monda-Amaya (2001) found that some general and special educators promoted an accepting classroom climate by eating lunch with small groups of students, or playing with them at recess, so that they would get to know and develop a relationship with each of them. Other teachers reported that having open classroom discussions on issues of concern to the students reduced conflict and facilitated group problem solving. As students develop a greater understanding of each other's strengths, challenges, and desires, they will have excellent suggestions regarding activities that can be added to the outdoor environment or how to modify existing outdoor activities and games so that everyone can be included.

The outside environment provides rich opportunities for peer interactions. Students with special needs should have access to a variety of activities that challenge them and encourage interactions among peers. Outdoor play allows students a level of comfort and freedom not found in the classroom, which, in turn, builds confidence and a sense of well-being. For students with special needs to benefit from outdoor environments, adaptations must be identified and created. Such adaptations open the door to learning, interactions with peers, increased independence, and a more active participation in all classroom activities.

For Further Reading:

Morris, L. R. (1989). *Creative play activities for children with disabilities* (2nd ed.). Champaign, IL: Human Kinetics Books.

Salend, S. J. (2001). *Creating inclusive classrooms* (4th ed.). Upper Saddle River, NJ: Merrill/Prentice-Hall.

Web sites:

www.cec.sped.org
Council for Exceptional Children. This Web site offers information and valuable links to resources and services.

www.gameskidsplay.net
The Web site offers an extensive list of play activities and games with rules. It includes many traditional games.

www.gamekids.com
Children may exchange ideas for games and activities.

www.access-board.gov/ada-aba.htm
Overview of the U.S. Access Board guidelines, published under the Americans With Disabilities Act and the Architectural Barriers Act, as it relates to play areas.

www.indiana.edu/%7enca/playground/play.htm
National Center on Accessibility guide to assist in creating inclusive play environments for children with and without disabilities.

References

Bergen, D. (1993). Facilitating friendship development in inclusion classrooms. *Childhood Education, 69*, 234-236.

Biklin, D. (1992). *Schooling without labels.* Philadelphia: Temple University Press.

Buchanan, M., & Cooney, M. (2000). Play at home, play in the classroom. *Young Exceptional Children, 3*, 9-15.

Covert, S. (1995). Elementary school inclusion that works. *Counterpoint, 15*, 1, 4.

Erwin, E. J., & Schreiber, R. (1999). Creating supports for young children with disabilities in natural environments. *Early Childhood Education Journal, 26*, 167-172.

Esposito, B. Gi., & Koorland, M. A. (1989). Play behavior of hearing impaired children: Integrated or segregated settings. *Exceptional Children, 55*, 412-419.

Flynn, L., & Kieff, J. E. (2002). Including EVERYONE in outdoor play. *Young Children, 57*(3), 20-26.

Haager, D., & Vaughn, S. (1995). Parent, teacher, and self-reports of the social competence of students with learning disabilities. *Journal of Learning Disabilities, 28*, 205-215.

Hughes, F. P. (1999). *Children, play, & development* (3rd ed.). Needham Heights, MA: Allyn and Bacon.

Jenkins, J. R., Odom, S. L., & Speltz, M. L. (1989). Effects of social integration on preschool children with handicaps. *Exceptional Children, 55*, 420-428.

Kohl, F. L., & Beckman, P. J. (1984). A comparison

of handicapped and non-handicapped preschoolers' interactions across classroom activities. *Journal of the Division of Early Childhood, 8,* 49-56.

Lamorey, S., & Bricker, D. D. (1993). Integrated programs: Effects on young children and their parents. In C. A. Peck, S. L. Odom, & D. D. Bricker (Eds.), *Integrating young children with disabilities into community programs* (pp. 249-270). Baltimore: Paul H. Brookes.

Li, A. K. F. (1985). Toward more elaborate pretend play. *Mental Retardation, 23,* 131-136.

Margalit, M. (1994). *Loneliness among children with special needs: Theory, research, coping, and intervention.* New York: Springer-Verlag.

Pavri, S. (2001). Loneliness in children with disabilities: How teachers can help. *Teaching Exceptional Children, 33*(6), 52-58.

Pavri, S., & Monda-Amaya, L. (2001). Social supports in inclusive schools: Student and teacher perspectives. *Exceptional Children, 67,* 391-411.

Pickett, P. L., Griffith, P. L., & Rogers-Adkinson, D. (1993). Integration of preschoolers with severe disabilities into day care. *Early Education and Development, 4,* 54-58.

Pugmire-Stoy, M. C. (1992). *Spontaneous play in early childhood.* Albany, NY: Delmar.

Stainback, W., & Stainback, S. (1990). *Support networks for inclusive schooling.* Baltimore: Paul H. Brookes.

CHAPTER 4

Creating Community and Resolving Conflicts

Laurie S. Frank

Laurie S. Frank is a former public school teacher who has worked in the adventure/experiential field for more than 20 years. She now works with schools and nonprofits to create collaborative learning communities.

A few summers ago, we were sitting on our front porch watching a group of children playing a classic neighborhood game—Kick the Can. Our first reaction was one of surprise; we had not encountered this game since our own childhoods, and children these days seemed so involved in structured free-time activities that it was unusual to see them playing together without a referee or umpire to deal with the eventual disputes that would arise.

The game unfolded like so many others. They played for about 20 minutes before the first conflict surfaced. It was fascinating to witness the arguments, raised voices, and even tears develop with no intervention by anyone over the age of about 13. Some of the children took on the role of mediator while others sat back and listened. Still others argued for their position. After about 10 minutes, the group arrived at a solution and continued their game. Twenty minutes later, the next conflict surfaced and the cycle of argument, mediation, and compromise started again.

These children were not just involved in a game. Their play was a learning experience that included the key conflict resolution skills of active listening, expressing feelings, identifying the problem, brainstorming, and looking for win-win solutions. These are skills that are best learned through experience. An adult-centered lecture or discussion does not provide the necessary practice that helps children learn and maintain these skills.

Conflict Resolution in Schools and Programs

In our schools and programs, conflicts and their resolution often are short-circuited by adults. This occurs for a variety of reasons: Our own discomfort with conflict, outside pressure from administration and peers to keep one's classroom "under control," a desire to rescue our students from difficult situations and emotional upset, a philosophy that the control and power in a classroom rests solely with the teacher, and even a belief that social/emotional learning detracts from covering academic content.

Yet, how do children learn how to resolve conflicts if the adults do not allow them to work through them? Conflicts happen, but they do not necessarily get resolved unless they are given attention. The goal of conflict resolution "is not to eliminate conflict," but rather to "help children learn from conflict, use it constructively and avoid its destructive aspects" (Kreidler & Furlong, 1996, p. 4). To achieve the goal of resolution, it is necessary to create a safe and respectful environment in which to disagree, and to teach the necessary skills.

Creating a safe and caring community provides the foundation for true conflict resolution by building essential connections among students. With this approach, children feel more motivated to resolve conflict, and many conflicts are even prevented due to the added values of respect and safety that go hand-in-hand with community building. Alfie Kohn (1996) defines community in this way:

Community . . . is a place in which students feel cared about and are encouraged to care about each other. They experience a sense of being valued and respected; the children matter to one another and to the teacher. They have come to think in the plural: they feel connected to each other; they are part of us. (p. 101)

Adventure Education and Community Building

As creating this sense of connection and community does not always happen automatically, programs have been created to help develop it. Programs that involve unstructured outside play allow students to put these skills into practice. One example is Adventure Education, which is uniquely suited as a tool for teaching conflict resolution skills. With some guided instruction, practice, and mediation from adults, children can learn essential life skills. In the meantime, the playground becomes a kinder, more caring place.

Adventure Education has its roots in the Outward Bound movement and can be loosely defined as "not knowing what's going to happen next." Smith, Roland, Havens, and Hoyt (1992) describe adventure as present "in many tasks that involve newness, risk, trust, sharing, and exploring the unknown" (p. 12). It can be found in a raft on a raging river or when picking up a worm. It can be experienced while rock climbing, or when starting a conversation with a potential new friend.

Adventure is everywhere, and is especially present in children's play. This natural tendency can be harnessed to create a sense of community and teach conflict resolution skills. Bower (1998) calls this Adventure Play (1998), which is highlighted by eight characteristics:

- Focuses on cooperation more than competition
- Challenges the individual to try new behaviors and new skills
- Encourages small groups of children to work together
- Promotes exploration and enjoyment of the environment

- Involves all players and does not eliminate anyone
- Offers opportunities for everyone at their own skill level
- Does not highlight certain players as better or less skilled than others
- Is creative and fun. (p. 3)

Using adventure to create community and teach conflict resolution taps into the innate tendencies of children. Together, they can explore concepts, learn skills, and play while discovering "what is going to happen next."

Adventure Techniques

Intentionally creating community through adventure requires the teacher to:

- **Create community norms** with the children
- Present activities in a careful **sequence**
- Address and teach topics for **conflict resolution skill-building**
- **Facilitate** rather than lecture.

Create Community Norms

A community cannot exist without norms. These unwritten rules are created whether we choose them or not. Thus, it is important to be intentional about creating norms; otherwise, the unintended ones can become the way the community operates.

Every classroom and program has rules that reflect organizational and physical safety policies. These are stated up front so that everyone is aware of how the teacher envisions optimal functioning for the class. In addition to these basic rules, it is important to have discussions about how people treat each other so that the class is an emotionally safe and respectful place. Younger children can discuss what it means to be kind and a good friend, while older students can delve into the meaning of respect. This is an ongoing discussion that begins on the first day, with each subsequent discussion and teachable moment getting more specific, clarifying concepts and helping to bring norms into clearer focus.

One formal version of group norms is called a Full Value Contract. This phrase, coined by Project Adventure in the 1980s, stresses the idea that everyone in the community is of equal (and full) value. The "contract" can be a written document that is created by the group and posted on the wall, ready to be referred to when necessary. It can be a life-size tracing of a person, known as a "Peaceable Being" (Kreidler & Furlong, 1996, p. 14), that includes words about how people want to be treated that are written on the inside of the silhouette. It can even be a legal-looking contract that each person is asked to sign.

Whether formal or informal, intentionally creating group norms is an essential part of community building.

Present Activities in a Sequence

When people come together for the first time, a general feeling of both excitement and anxiety exists. Everyone is wondering whether or not they will be accepted, and if they belong. Given that belonging is a basic human need (Glasser, 1986), it is essential that teachers create a welcoming environment where everyone feels invited and feels they belong. A sense of belonging is a basic building block of trust, which is emphasized later in the sequence. Adventure Education attempts to address this need through a series of icebreaker activities. Names are learned, and children are given an opportunity to share personal information about hobbies, pets, number of siblings, etc. It is a time to introduce oneself and meet others.

Once students feel more comfortable, then it is possible to ease into De-inhibitizer Activities. Like the name suggests, these activities help break down barriers and ask participants to share more of themselves by taking some risks. These risks can take the form of being put on the spot by being in the middle of the circle during a game, touching someone else, or acting silly. If children have opportunities to take some risks in a supportive environment, trust can continue to grow within the group.

The next step in the sequence is a focus on Trust. Trust permeates everything in a community, and it is an essential ingredient for conflict resolution. Children are ready for dealing with issues of trust when they show kindness toward others, demonstrate that they care if someone gets hurt, are able to laugh with (and not at) others, and have enough self-control to take the safety of others seriously. Trust is not something to be taken lightly and can just as easily be broken as built. It is important to remember that the activities do not, in themselves, build trust. It is what people do during the activities that builds (or breaks) trust.

Problem Solving Initiatives allow students to formally practice skills they have been learning along the way. Conflict is more apt to appear during these activities because the teacher now simply states the basic rules and students are required to solve the problem. Up to this point, the rules had been very clear, and the teacher was mainly responsible for making sure they were followed.

The difference between using these activities to teach concepts and pure recreation lies in the focus and discussion topics that are part of the learning scheme. Each activity can have a "point," so that the lessons build on one another. Consequently, community building and conflict resolution skill building can take place simultaneously.

It is the process, rather than the task, that is important. The discussion/focus topics can be explored using activities that are commonly played in classrooms and programs around the country. The way to begin is to decide if the activity you choose fits the Adventure Play criteria and is in the appropriate sequence for the group.

Build Conflict Resolution Skills

Conflict naturally happens, but resolution does not. An individual's ability to resolve conflict depends upon myriad factors: ability to listen, capacity to identify feelings, willingness to deal with uncomfortable situations, recognition of a conflict situation, capacity to deal with anger, and depth of a conflict resolution "toolbox" that gives one a variety of strategies to use when involved in a conflict situation.

If a child cannot tell the difference between frustration and rage, and the only tool he or she has to deal with conflict is hitting, then a frustrating situation can become quickly violent. The community building process offers both the chance to establish trusting relationships that allow conflict to be resolved, and a vehicle to directly teach conflict resolution processes and strategies. At first, the focus is creating a sense of inclusion and belonging. During this time, it makes sense to teach students how to actively listen to each other by using the skills of looking at the speaker, nodding to show you are attentive, and asking clarifying questions. Aside from helping students connect, active listening is a basic conflict resolution skill. A simple activity to teach listening skills is a call and response, whereby a rhythm is established, one person calls out a phrase, and everyone repeats it. Check to see if people are looking at the person who is speaking. This can be followed with short (one minute) speeches that permit students to formally practice their active listening skills.

Appreciating diversity is a building block of conflict resolution, because it helps people understand those who are different from them, thus opening up communication avenues that might have been closed. Activities that ask students to share information about themselves and their family are a good start in exposing children to different perspectives. Honoring the diversity in the class can become a group norm that helps propel the class forward in their community-building efforts.

In his landmark book *Emotional Intelligence*, Daniel Goleman (1995) states, "The emotional faculty guides our moment-to-moment decisions, working hand-in-hand with the rational mind, enabling—or disabling—thought itself" (p. 28). In other words, emotions play a central role in being able to think rationally, and thus have the ability to resolve conflicts. It takes a rational mind partnered with a feelings vocabulary to work effectively through a conflict. One must be able to identify a range of feelings, and then express those feelings in a constructive way. Most children come equipped with "mad, sad, glad" and little else. Yet even very young children can tell the difference between "glad" and "thrilled" if given the time to learn and connect the words with the feelings. Being "annoyed" with Kelly is far different from being "infuriated," and a conflict will play out differently depending upon how the child interprets his or her feelings.

Tied to emotional literacy is the ability to manage anger and de-escalate a conflict. We often get on the "conflict escalator" (Kreidler & Furlong, 1996, p. 241) in a kind of tit-for-tat dynamic. Tanya finds Sarah's ball and picks it up; Sarah tries to grab it; Tanya makes a face at Sarah as she pulls away; Sarah calls Tanya a name; Tanya kicks Sarah; Sarah pulls Tanya's hair, and so on. Physical violence has erupted from a tossed ball. Teaching how to de-escalate conflict paves the way for resolution. Until one is in a rational state of mind, however, the conflict cannot be resolved. The best situation is when people choose to stay off the conflict escalator altogether. Second best is a "cooling off period" before the parties attempt their resolution. Children require guidance and practice to achieve this status.

Another step in learning conflict resolution is to enlarge one's toolbox of resolution strategies. Kreidler and Furlong (1996, p. 252) suggest some useful strategies: Learning how to make a peace offering or saying "sorry" can stop a conflict in its tracks. Knowing how to compromise and talk it out can help people work through a conflict situation. Even deciding to skip it can be a practical strategy, as a way to learn how to "pick one's battles."

The Mediation Center in Asheville, North Carolina (Kreidler & Furlong, 1996), offers a simple way to teach this to children and adults alike:

- **A**sk what the problem is
- **B**rainstorm possible solutions
- **C**hoose the best solution
- **D**o it. (p. 256)

All of these skills can be taught through adventure activities and discussion.

Facilitate the Process

The activities used to build community and teach conflict resolution do not accomplish these goals in and of themselves. Playing a game, while fun, may not teach the desired skills. To do this takes facilitation by the teacher.

Frequently, adults are tempted to manipulate the process so that children "get it." Unfortunately, this system has not proven to be successful. The more opportunities people have to interact with ideas that are new and different, the more they will be able to make sense of these concepts for themselves. Learning takes time. To tell a child something does not mean that he or she learns it.

Adventure Education is a way to give people an opportunity to interact with ideas—to explore, if you will. A way to do this is to present an activity, and then take time to reflect upon what lessons might have been learned when doing the activity. This process, called the Experiential Learning Cycle, is well-articulated by Bower (1998):

- Identify a conflict resolution concept/skill
- Choose an activity to highlight the concept/skill
- State the concept/skill at the beginning of the activity
- After the activity, reflect on:
  what happened during the activity,
  what learning we can get from this activity, and
  how we will apply it in class and in the rest of our lives (processing).

The Role of Unstructured Outdoor Play

Teaching the skills of conflict resolution is honorable, but the skills are useless if not practiced outside of the actual learning situation. Unstructured outdoor play is a natural venue for children to practice these skills. Recess time is frequently a time of great frustration for the supervising adults and students alike. Children are regularly tattling or getting into out-and-out fights. Adults are then seen in the role of dealing punishment.

In a discussion of play and sectarianism in Northern Ireland, an organization known as Games Not Names shares that, "Play is universal and as children play it helps them not only to realize their own potential, but to acquire a knowledge of adult life and the social values of the society in which they live" (Games Not Names, n.d., p. 3). The more adults allow children the freedom to play unencumbered, the more likely they will learn from those play opportunities.

This is not to say that children should be left to their own devices. Children may not yet have the skills to resolve the conflicts that arise. One's aim, however, is to support the children to use the skills they possess, and to continue to teach the ones they still need. As children learn the necessary skills, and become better equipped to solve their own disputes, it is the responsibility of the adult to remind and encourage them to use those skills. The more adults do for the children, the less that children will do for themselves. Learning to become adept at resolving conflicts takes constant practice, and skilled facilitation by the adults.

Summary

Unstructured outdoor play is a natural vehicle through which children can learn and practice life skills, such as conflict resolution. They do not necessarily learn these skills on their own, however. Changing recess time from an exercise in tattling and fighting to a time when children resolve their conflicts peacefully is a gradual process, and requires teaching necessary skills. Conflict resolution also takes place within the context of relationships. People must care enough to want to resolve the conflicts that arise; these feelings can be supported by intentionally creating a sense of community built on belonging and trust.

Adventure Education is a tool that can create community and teach conflict resolution skills simultaneously. It includes creating community norms, presenting activities in a sequence, teaching topics for conflict resolution, and facilitating the process with students. Activities are presented and then processed, using an Experiential Learning Cycle model, so that children can apply their skills outside of the learning environment.

A perfect practice arena is the playground, where children can play without excessive restrictions. At first, adults take on most of the responsibility to facilitate the resolution of the inevitable conflicts that occur. As children learn the necessary skills, they are supported and encouraged by the adults to use them to resolve their own conflicts on the playground.

References

Bower, N. M. (1998). *Adventure play.* Needham Heights, MA: Simon & Schuster.

Games Not Names. (n.d.). Belfast, Northern Ireland: PlayBoard.

Glasser, W. (1986). *Control theory in the classroom.* New York: Harpers and Row.

Goleman, D. (1995). *Emotional intelligence.* New York: Bantam Books.

Kohn, A. (1996). *Beyond discipline: From compliance to community.* Alexandria, VA: Association for Supervision and Curriculum Development.

Kreidler, W. J., & Furlong, L. (1996). *Adventures in peacemaking: A conflict resolution activity guide.* Hamilton, MA: Project Adventure, Inc.

Smith, T. E., Roland, C. C., Havens, M. D., & Hoyt, J. A. (1992). *The theory and practice of challenge education.* Dubuque, IA: Kendall/Hunt Publishing Company.

CHAPTER 5

Becoming an Advocate for Play in the Elementary and Middle School Years

Sandra J. Stone

Sandra J. Stone is a Professor of Literacy and Early Childhood in the College of Education at Northern Arizona University.

In the name of academic excellence, children have too long endured the absence of play, both indoors and outdoors. We see an erosion of quality play time for all children, because society continues to focus on a linear curriculum with an emphasis on transmitting informational facts (Elkind, 1990; Fromberg, 2002). Sutton-Smith (1988) suggests that these linear approaches in U.S. schools further decrease children's outdoor play and recess opportunities. If we are to be true advocates for children, then we must be outspoken advocates for play. Educators must let their voices be heard. We must not succumb to the narrow definition of "learning" that undervalues or eliminates play as a curricular tool (Bergen, 1988).

Play is deemed by many experts as vitally important to the growth of the whole child (Bergen, 1988; Bruner, 1983; Elkind, 1981; Fein, 1986; Fromberg, 2002; Piaget, 1962; Vygotsky, 1976). The Association for Childhood Education International (ACEI) takes a strong position on play. ACEI "recognizes the need for children of all ages to play and affirms the essential role of play in children's lives.... ACEI supports all adults who respect, understand, and advocate legitimizing play as an essential pathway to learning for all children" (Isenberg & Quisenberry, 2002, p. 33). Furthermore, ACEI believes that play is an essential and integral part of healthy growth for children of all ages. Frost (1992) calls play an "indispensable element in child development. It is the child's natural process of learning and development and, consequently, a critical ingredient in the educative process" (p. 19). As nonlinear learning, play allows children to construct meaning through interactions with others and the physical world (Fromberg, 2002). Fromberg suggests that play creates nonlinear environments, which help to build caring communities consisting of responsible and independent members who are empowered to play with ideas in order to make meaningful connections. Brain research also supports the importance of play in creating the neurological connections necessary for learning (Jensen, 2000). Indoor and outdoor play offers numerous opportunities for children to grow and develop physically, cognitively, socially, and emotionally (Frost, Wortham, & Reifel, 2001; McGinnis, 2002; Rivkin, 1995). It is important that outdoor play be offered by all school programs for children of all ages and abilities (Isenberg & Quisenberry, 2002).

With such strong proponents of play as a curricular choice, one would think that play would enjoy a place of honor in our schools and society—that children would participate in play as a "cherished" component of appropriate practice. What we find across the United

---

Note: This chapter is based on the author's article "Wanted: Advocates for Play in the Primary Grades" published in 1995 in *Young Children, 50*(6), 45-54.

States, however, is that educators have deliberately or unwittingly sacrificed play in their endeavors to reach prescribed academic goals. Even teachers who know the importance of play to a child's development find themselves on the defensive when questioned about play, in and out of their classrooms. We have become embarrassed to give time and place to play because of "more important" curricular priorities. To those who value play and understand its critical importance to the growth and development of children, the question thus becomes how do we empower ourselves to become true advocates of play?

Recognizing What Play Is

First, we must be able to recognize play in order to promote and nurture it. Play is defined as intrinsically motivated, freely chosen, process-oriented over product, non-literal, and enjoyable (Johnson, Christie, & Yawkey, 1999). Although play is "hands-on learning," hands-on learning is not always play. Teachers must not assume that active learning, even outdoor learning, constitutes play. Educators should know the difference and provide for both. Since play is non-literal, internal reality takes precedence over external reality. "This 'as if' stance allows children to escape the constraints of here and now and experiment with new possibilities" (Johnson et al., 1999, p. 16).

In order to recognize play, looking at play types is helpful. Smilansky's (1968) adaptation of Piaget's (1962) cognitive play categories are standard for play observers. There are four categories: functional, constructive, dramatic, and games with rules.

Functional Play. Functional play is when the child runs, jumps, splashes in water, or repetitively manipulates objects or materials. In functional play, the child repeats muscle movements with or without objects just for the sake of movement. In outdoor play, teachers can see many forms of functional play: children bouncing a ball over and over again, running with no goal in mind, swinging back and forth on a swing, rolling a rock over and over again in her hand, or engaging in "rough and tumble

play" (for a further discussion on rough and tumble play, see Chapter 10). All these actions are forms of functional play. Children gain great pleasure in playing in and with the environment, not for a product but for the sheer enjoyment of movement. Although functional play decreases as children grow older, it still plays an important role in their lives.

Constructive Play. Constructive play is when children use objects or materials to make things. They create, construct, and solve problems. In constructive play, children build with Legos and wood. They make things with clay, paint, paper, and even mud and sand. One can see outdoor constructive play when children build a fort with wood and boxes on an adventure playground, draw with chalk on a sidewalk, and create rivers and mountains with sand and dirt.

Dramatic Play. Dramatic play is when children role-play or make pretend transformations. Dramatic play becomes sociodramatic play when children role-play together. In dramatic play, a child may pretend she is a superhero. Or, he may transform a box into a car, a tree into a safe haven, a stick into a wand, or himself into a monster. In sociodramatic play, the child is given multiple opportunities to be social as well as play out her emotions. She is able to problem solve and use her imagination and creativity. Thus, dramatic play's importance for the preadolescent and adolescent child should not be underestimated and should be given high priority for her healthy development.

Games With Rules. Games with rules involve the type of play wherein children make or use rules to play games. These may be simple or complex rules that are pre-established by the players. Examples of games with rules are tag, hide-and-seek, dodge ball, hopscotch, and football. Children develop or use rules to establish "how the play is supposed to go." Games with rules are frequent and important modes of play for preadolescent and adolescent children, and they support a child's development as he orders his world for consistency, fairness, stability, and predictability (Stone, 1993).

Although children will engage in constructive and dramatic games and games with rules more frequently than functional play, all four types of play are important for the development of children in the elementary and middle school years. Knowing the types of children's play will help educators not only recognize forms of play when they see it, but also help them facilitate, honor, and plan for play's place in the outdoor environment. Outdoor play areas should provide for all types of play.

Verbalizing Our Knowledge of the Benefits/Values of Play

To be a true advocate of children's play, a teacher must be able to verbalize her knowledge about the values of play. Stone (1993) notes that the "research on the values of play is formidable. In fact, there is so much evidence of play's overall benefits that to provide an 'education' without play seems ludicrous" (p. 7). Knowledge of the values of play can empower a teacher to promote play outdoors as well as in the classroom (Almy, 1984; Athey, 1984; Bruner, 1983; Fein, 1986; Fromberg, 2002; Frost et al., 2001; Stone, 1995; Vygotsky, 1976).

First, play creates a natural learning environment. Wassermann (1992) describes five benefits of play. Children are able to: generate (create) something new, take risks, avoid the fear of failure, be autonomous, and actively engage their minds and bodies (p. 135). Play provides the natural and experiential learning that supports the child's construction of his own knowledge of the world and his place in it. It significantly affects the development of the whole child. Within play's natural learning environment, children develop cognitively, socially, emotionally, and physically.

Cognitive Development. Research substantiates a strong relationship between play and cognitive development. Play has a crucial role in developing abstract thought in young children and continues to afford children of all ages the opportunity to use divergent thinking (Pepler, 1982). Children

conduct research to find solutions to problems as they play. If a child is building a structure outside, he explores many ways to keep the structure from falling over. Each problem he encounters in constructive play gives him an opportunity to think divergently and find solutions.

Play is the natural place for children to express creativity. Children create, invent, and design as they draw, build, and dramatize. In constructive play, the child sculpts with mud and sand, designs with paint, and constructs with wood and natural materials—all expressions of the child's creativity. In dramatic play, the "child is able to take a multitude of experiences and lace them together into new ones, which represents a monument to her creativity" (Stone, 1993, p. 120).

Play encourages problem-solving. Problems encountered in play represent real, thus meaningful, problems to children (Tegano, Sawyers, & Moran, 1989). Real problems provide the motivation to engage in the problem-solving process. Providing a play context for children is an effective way to help children develop problem-solving skills across all dimensions naturally. Instead of talking through problems, children play through problems for solutions. Tegano, Sawyers, and Moran (1989) note that "children who are encouraged to find and 'play' with their problems (trying out various solutions) are more apt to learn generalizable skills and be better equipped to cope with real life problems" (p. 97).

Play also provides an avenue for concept development, through which children test out and revise their concepts of the world. In mud play, the child develops concepts of mass, volume, and the nature of change. The child develops concepts of air pressure, gravitation, and aerodynamics when he plays with kites. Scientific concepts such as force, gravity, and balance are discovered as a child builds shelters with raw or recycled materials.

Perspective-taking is a cognitive process that often takes place during sociodramatic play. The child learns how to see the world from another's point of view as she takes on the roles of different characters. The social interaction also allows her to see things from her friend's point of view. Being able to see something from another's point of view is a critical life skill facilitated by play.

Play also provides a rich environment for language development. As a child interacts with others, he must communicate meaning as well as develop narrative language, as demonstrated in sociodramatic play and games with rules. Especially valuable to his language development is that in play, the new words are tied to meaning and experiences enacted or engaged in by the child.

Social Development. Play is the primary mode for children's social development (Rubin, 1980). Play encourages social interaction. Children learn how to negotiate, resolve conflicts, solve problems, get along with each other, take turns, be patient, cooperate, and share. Play also helps children understand concepts of fairness and competition.

Even though perspective-taking is a cognitive skill, it is also vital to a child's social development. Play supports children in the "decentering" process. This is especially important as children learn to deal with their friends' feelings and attitudes.

Play contributes to children's social competence by giving them the opportunity to be social. It also provides children with an arena in which to practice social conventions, and with the freedom to accept or reject those conventions. Through play, children develop friendships and learn that someone else values them.

Emotional Development. Play is a medium whereby children can express their feelings as well as learn to cope with them. Through play, children have an outlet for expressing feelings of happiness, sadness, anger, or worry. In this world of play, these feelings can be explored and expressed freely because the feelings are not in the "real world." In pretend play, the feelings can be understood and worked out. Play provides this safe context for emotional development. A child can repeatedly revisit an unsettling incident, such as seeing someone hurt on the playground. He replays the scene until he is able to cope with his feelings of fear. In this sense, play softens the realities of the world. Play is a risk-free environment where unpleasant experiences can be worked out.

Elkind (1981) suggests that play is also a release from the stresses children face. Physiological evidence links play with anxiety reduction (Barnett & Storm, 1981). In our hurried society, play gives children a way to escape and be in control of their world, their thoughts, and their feelings.

Physical Development. Outdoor play is the primary way children develop physically. Play provides opportunities for both fine and gross motor development. Children can test out their balancing systems as they do acrobatics, they can develop a command of their bodies as they skip and hop, and they can learn to judge distances as they jump and throw. Play also gives children opportunities to develop hand-eye coordination. As children play, they test out their bodies to see how they best function. And, as children develop a command of their bodies, play helps them feel physically "confident, secure, and self-assured" (Isenberg & Quisenberry, 2002, p. 34).

Knowing the cognitive, social, emotional, and physical benefits of play to the development of children is essential if educators are to be advocates for children's play. We need to be able to verbalize our knowledge of the value of play to parents, teachers, and administrators.

Being "Open" Advocates for Play

Knowing what play is, as well as the different types and benefits of play, can empower us to be "open" advocates for play. No longer do we have to hide play in our curriculum, give only cursory "free time" for children to play, or be embarrassed when someone sees our children playing. Equipped with the knowledge of the value of play, educators can not only allow play to occur indoors and outdoors, but even vigorously plan for it.

Posting the benefits of play in a prominent place (see Figure 1) lets parents and colleagues, and, most of all, your children know that "Play is valued here!" It is equally important to demonstrate that learning is taking place. We can display evidence of things children have invented or solved and use anecdotal records to substantiate times of negotiation, planning, and sharing. Teachers may take photographs of children's creations or videotape the dramatizations.

Vivid examples of the benefits of play will further support the position that play is valuable, but even more important, this information will help guide our instructional decisions as we become astute observers of what is happening during outdoor play.

Another way to become an "open" advocate of play is to inform others. We can share timely articles with colleagues, schedule discussion groups with interested teachers and parents, and exchange valuable play experiences with each other.

Involving Parents

Parents can be valued partners in creating and supporting quality outdoor play experiences for their children. A class newsletter sent to parents can periodically highlight the importance of children's indoor and outdoor play as a useful educational tool. At informative parent meetings planned throughout the year, when we may normally discuss literacy development and math strategies, we also can share how outdoor play supports children's learning, growth, and development.

Teachers upgrade the importance of play by bringing it into the context of parent conferences. Letting parents see how outdoor play is integrated into our curriculum and how we use play to help each child in his development is valuable. This can be done by sharing each child's play experiences that document growth, for example, in imagination, problem solving, negotiation, and physical development.

The Benefits of Play

Emotional
- Acts as a medium for expressing thoughts/feelings
- Softens the realities of the world
- Serves as a risk-free environment
- Releases children's stress
- Decreases children's anxiety
- Builds well-being/self-concepts

Physical
- Motor development
- Balancing of systems
- Body command
- Distance judgment
- Hand-eye coordination
- Testing of bodies
- Self-assurance

Cognitive
- Abstract thought
- Divergent thinking
- Creativity
- Problem solving
- Concept development
- Perspective taking
- Language development

Social
- Decentering
- Practicing of social patterns
- Encouraging social interaction
- Learning to get along

Figure 1

We want to involve parents in planning outdoor play experiences at home or on the playground. Inviting parents to observe or participate in the children's outdoor play and having them as partners will strengthen our advocacy role.

Investigating Ways You Can Integrate Outdoor Play Into the Curriculum

Play's integration into the curriculum can be done by creating a variety of outdoor play experiences, props, and games (Bogdanoff & Dolch, 1979; Henniger, 1993; Stone, 1995/1996). Wassermann (1992) suggests that "virtually every important concept to be taught—whether it be at the primary, intermediate or graduate level or whether it be in science, math, economics or business management—can be taught through the medium of serious play" (p. 137). In the science and social studies areas, a few chicken bones become the objects of an outside archaeology dig, a pond becomes a biological collection site, and chalk becomes the tool for drawing various dinosaurs to scale on the basketball court. In the outdoors, children can re-create sand replicas of pyramids, make fossils, and discover changes in matter. They can play outdoor games typical of the time period of the literature book *Sarah, Plain and Tall* (MacLachlan, 1985). Children may create their own outdoor play areas based on their interests. During this process, the children will invent, design, problem solve, and plan—all of which constitute higher order

thinking skills. The possibilities are endless for outdoor play and learning.

Outdoor play may be infused into all the content areas of an integrated curriculum: setting up an outdoor plant store when studying economics, creating a rain forest with real plants when studying the environment, and providing simple props for re-creating history through outdoor socio-dramatic play. With a few props, children become pioneers, archaeologists, biologists, and astronauts.

As we evaluate our outdoor play environment, let's look at it with "playful" eyes. We can ask ourselves, "Where can outdoor play be added to support my children's cognitive, social, emotional, and physical growth?" We also should remember that outdoor play and outdoor learning may be two separate, yet important, experiences. Outdoor experiences can be play only as long as they meet the criteria for play. As previously stated, play should be intrinsically motivated, freely chosen, process-oriented over product, non-literal, and enjoyable (Johnson et al., 1999). If these criteria are not met, then the outdoor experiences may be "meaningful learning," but not play. Too often, well-

When playing out-of-doors, seasonal changes provide children with a variety of learning and play opportunities.

defined teacher-initiated experiences become learning projects rather than creative play construction by the children (Stone, 1993). Again, the knowledgeable teacher must know the difference and adequately provide for both outdoor play and outdoor learning.

Creating Quality Time for Play

When planning for outdoor play, it is crucial to provide enough time—at least 30 minutes—for play to evolve. However we choose to provide for play, whether integrated into the curriculum or given a block of time, we want to make sure the time is sufficient for quality play to take place.

Honoring Children's Play

To be an advocate for play also means to honor children's play. This is done not only by providing time for play, but also by planning for and encouraging play. A teacher who plans for play is most likely to encourage continued play. We can encourage play by expressing pleasure in the children's play, admiring an intricately constructed fort, or agreeing to be scorekeeper for a game. Honoring children's play involves respect for the process. Teachers who do not understand the value of play will communicate their non-valuing feelings by retreating from or ignoring the play. A teacher who does not honor play may say to herself, "The children are just playing. While they are 'busy,' I will do more important things." A teacher who honors play encourages children to play by involving himself in the play as an observer, supporter, or participant.

Creating "Play" Support Groups

While play is acceptable for young children, advocating play in the elementary and middle years (8- to 12-year-olds) is, indeed, a challenge. We need to find colleagues in our schools, school districts, or the wider educational community who also value play for older children. A support group will strengthen our roles as advocates. Many voices are better than one isolated voice. Support groups share information, exchange ideas, and confirm beliefs. A support group does not have to be large. A group can be as small as two people and as many as 100. The important thing is to have someone who supports our position of advocacy for play.

Becoming an advocate for play in the intermediate years is not an easy role. Critics lie in wait to attack such frivolous use of time in public schools. To keep outdoor play in the schools where it exists and to return play to schools void of play will require courageous people to step forward (Stone, 1995).

References

Almy, M. (1984). A child's right to play. *Childhood Education, 60*, 350.

Athey, I. (1984). Contributions of play to development. In T. D. Yawkey & A. D. Pellegrini (Eds.), *Child's play: Developmental and applied* (pp. 9-27). Hillsdale, NJ: Erlbaum.

Barnett, L. A., & Storm, B. (1981). Play, pleasure, and pain: The reduction of anxiety through play. *Leisure Sciences, 4*, 161-175.

Bergen, D. (Ed.). (1988). *Play as a medium for learning and development.* Portsmouth, NH: Heinemann.

Bogdanoff, R. F., & Dolch, E. T. (1979). Old games for young children: A link to our heritage. *Young Children, 34*(2), 37-45.

Bruner, J. (1983). Play, thought, and language. *Peabody Journal of Education, 60*(3), 60-69.

Elkind, D. (1981). *The hurried child: Growing up too fast too soon.* Menlo Park, CA: Addison-Wesley.

Elkind, D. (1990). Academic pressure-too much, too soon: The demise of play. In E. Klugman & S. Smilansky (Eds.), *Children's play and learning: Perspectives and policy implications* (pp. 3-17). New York: Teachers College Press.

Fein, G. (1986). The play of children. In G. Fein & M. Rivkin (Eds.), *The young child at play. Reviews of research, 4* (pp. vii-xiv). Washington, DC: National Association for the Education of Young Children.

Fromberg, D. P. (2002). *Play and meaning in early childhood education.* Boston: Allyn & Bacon.

Frost, J. L. (1992). *Play and playscapes.* Albany, NY: Delmar.

Frost, J., Wortham, S., & Reifel, S. (2001). *Play and child development.* Upper Saddle River, NJ: Merrill/Prentice-Hall.

Henniger, M. L. (1993). Enriching the outdoor play experience. *Childhood Education, 70,* 87-90.

Isenberg, J., & Quisenberry, N. (2002). Play: Essential for all children. *Childhood Education, 79,* 33-39.

Jensen, E. (2000). Moving with the brain in mind. *Educational Leadership, 58*(3), 34-37.

Johnson, J. E., Christie, J. F., & Yawkey, T. D. (1999). *Play and early childhood development.* Glenview, IL: ScottForesman.

MacLachlan, P. (1985). *Sarah, plain and tall.* New York: Harper & Row.

McGinnis, J. L. (2002). Enriching outdoor environments. *Young Children, 57*(3), 28.

Pepler, D. J. (1982). Play and divergent thinking. In D. J. Pepler & H. Rubin (Eds.), *Contributions to human development, Vol. 6. The play of children: Current theory and research* (pp. 64-78). Basel, Switzerland: Karger.

Piaget, J. (1962). *Play, dreams, and imitation in childhood.* New York: Norton.

Rivkin, M. S. (1995). *The great outdoors: Restoring children's right to play outside.* Washington, DC: National Association for the Education of Young Children.

Rubin, K. H. (1980). Fantasy play: Its role in the development of social skills and social cognition. In K. H. Rubin (Ed.), *Children's play* (pp. 69-84). San Francisco: Jossey-Bass.

Smilansky, S. (1968). *The effects of sociodramatic play on disadvantaged preschool children.* New York: Wiley.

Stone, S. J. (1993). *Playing: A kid's curriculum.* Glenview, IL: GoodYear Books.

Stone, S. J. (1995). Wanted: Advocates for play in the primary grades. *Young Children, 50*(6), 45-54.

Stone, S. J. (1995/1996). Integrating play into the curriculum. *Childhood Education, 72,* 104-107.

Sutton-Smith, B. (1988). Radicalizing childhood: The multivocal voice. In L. R. Williams & D. P. Fromberg (Eds.), *Defining the field of early childhood education* (pp. 77-140). Charlottesville, VA: W. Alton Jones Foundation.

Tegano, D. W., Sawyers, J. K., & Moran, J. D., III. (1989). Problem-finding and solving in play: The teacher's role. *Childhood Education, 66,* 92-97.

Vygotsky, L. S. (1976). Play and its role in the mental development of the child. In J. S. Bruner, A. Jolly, & K. Sylva (Eds.), *Play: Its role in development and evolution* (pp. 537-544). New York: Basic Books.

Wassermann, S. (1992). Serious play in the classroom. *Childhood Education, 68,* 133-139.

Section II

The Out-of-Doors: Development, Learning, and Play

CHAPTER 6

The Out-of-Doors and Development
A Good Match

Kathleen G. Burriss

*Kathleen G. Burriss is a Professor in the Department of Elementary
and Special Education at Middle Tennessee State University.*

Confused by self-doubt, plagued with forgetfulness, addicted to extreme fads, preoccupied with peer status, disturbed about physical development, aroused by physiological impulses, stimulated by mass media communication, confronted by daydreams, chafed by restrictions, loaded with purposeless energy, bored by routine, irked by social amenities, veneered with "wisecracks," insulated from responsibility, labeled with delinquency, obsessed with personal autonomy, but destined to years of economic dependency, early adolescents undergo a critical and frequently stormy period in their lives. (Illinois Junior High Education 1965, Illinois Junior High School Principals' Association, as cited in McGlasson, 1973, p. 7)

As they mature, preadolescents experience dramatic physical, social, emotional, and intellectual changes. In fact, with the exception of the first three years of life, more biological changes occur from age 10 to 14 than in any other period of life (Wiles & Bondi, 2001). These overt physiological changes frequently overshadow the significant emotional, social, and intellectual development experienced by young adolescents.

If aware of the particular developmental trends of this age, educators can plan learning experiences that build on children's strengths and nurture less emergent areas. The out-of-doors environment holds particular potential for mediating children's social, emotional, and intellectual learning in distinct ways not possible in the traditional indoor classroom. This chapter describes some developmental trends represented in 8- through 12-year-old children and explains how providing outdoor activities positively influences their learning and development.

Consider the Philosophy

Using the outdoors as a classroom does not have to be limited to activities that involve studying aspects of the outdoor environment (e.g., a study of trees, a garden project, or an entomological observation unit). The outdoor classroom is philosophically understood to extend upon and enrich all aspects of the learning process. The out-of-doors ensures a range of physical and personnel resources, provides a variety of opportunities for naturalistic inquiry, allows for observation and data collection, and holds the potential for uniquely aesthetic experiences. Children can explore a variety of outdoor locales, ranging from a construction site to an outdoor sculpture garden. At each location, experts can guide the students' inquiry while, at the same time, serving as adult community role models. Breaking away from the traditional indoor classroom format allows students to observe and gather a variety of information. Allowing students to interact with nonschool-related individuals supports development of different audience and communication styles. Finally, leaving behind the traditional indoor classroom grants students the chance to appreciate a variety of aesthetic experiences like rock formations, a reflective pond, or a planetarium.

Allowing children to observe their urban environment from the 50th floor of an observation deck, at street level, and from a subway provides learners with a unique opportunity to develop insight and appreciate the need for an aesthetic dimension to daily living. Frequently, it is such nontraditional elementary school experiences that motivate, inspire, and initiate students' creativity. Lifelong careers and avocations often generate from outdoor activities, as such experiences extend and enrich children's lives in personal ways. Also, the outdoor classroom contributes to the more formal indoor learning, which includes the academic disciplines of language arts, mathematics, science, and social studies.

The out-of-door classroom can provide a motivating and reflective setting for children's reading, writing, poetry, and journal entries. These activities can be pursued as a class, in small groups, or as individuals. The open nature of the outdoor classroom nurtures spontaneity, flexibility, and free expression. These attributes appeal to the older elementary and adolescent learner. In addition, the out-of-doors provides real-life opportunities with which to integrate curriculum. The indoor and outdoor environments are intricately related in terms of children's interests. If we are measuring, measure the slide; if we are estimating, predict the number of bricks used to build the school; if we are studying directions, record local signage; and if we are talking about recycling, build a compost pile. That is, think of the out-of-doors as an annex of the traditional classroom.

Begin With Development

Although the ways in which children intellectually, emotionally, and physically grow are uniquely individual, children do share some characteristics at particular ages. When educators understand the similarities among elementary and middle school children, they can plan instruction that builds on children's common behaviors and interests. Through no fault of their own, children in the later elementary years experience frustration in defining self-concept, difficulty in complying with authority, and anxiety about feeling accepted by others. As children become aware of themselves as individuals, they also become self-conscious and wonder how others perceive them (Girl Scout Council of Cumberland Valley, 2001). There is a strong emerging need for self-worth. Children want to understand self and feelings. Therefore, they need opportunities to develop and express autonomy and independence (Gilstrap, Bierman, & McKnight, 1992). As children struggle with emotional and physiological changes, their affiliation base broadens from the family to the peer group. With this social shift, the peer group becomes a source for standards and models of behavior. Although authority remains within the family, children want to make their own choices (Wiles & Bondi, 2001). Society's mobility has uprooted historical peer relationships (Wiles & Bondi, 2001), which has caused children stress. Thus, the school community becomes not simply a resource for academic learning, but also a framework for social and emotional guidance.

During the later elementary grades, children also begin to grow in their ability to think. They gradually shift from concrete to early formal mental activities (Gilstrap et al., 1992). However, they remain primarily in the concrete operation stage of development (Wiles & Bondi, 2001). During the concrete thinking stage (approximately 7 to 11 years of age), children acquire and begin to use components of logical thinking (Shaffer, 1999). Children are no longer fooled by or bound to physical appearances. They can rely on mental activity. They understand the basic properties of and relationships among objects and events in the everyday world. They can think abstractly (Wiles & Bondi, 2001). Therefore, children need both formal and informal situations to practice and improve their reasoning powers (Wiles & Bondi, 2001). Children are also becoming more effective at making inferences by observing others' behavior and the circumstances in which it occurs. However, the necessity for hands-on learning is not limited to the early childhood years. Although elementary and adolescent children can reason abstractly, they still benefit from engaging in authentic learning experiences. They apply mental activity "only to objects, situations, or events that are real or imaginable" (Shaffer, 1999, p. 239). That is, children "are likely to be accurate only for real objects that are (or have been) physically present" (p. 239). What this means is that while older children (11-12 years of age and beyond), who have moved to more formal mental activity, are capable of thinking abstractly, such thinking remains difficult without concrete experience and personal meaning. Therefore, for middle and later elementary children (4th through 7th grade), hands-on and relevant learning is as important as it is during the early childhood years.

In particular, when 7- to 11-year-old children perceive learning as useful, they demonstrate curiosity and an eager willingness to learn. They enjoy using skills to solve real-life problems (Wiles & Bondi, 2001). The out-of-doors offers great scope for such activities.

Outdoor learning activities promote the emotional and social development of pre-adolescents. The activities also can include academic goals that complement children's intellectual stage of development. For older children, this is particularly possible through studies related to the community. Planning outdoor activities that integrate the real world allows older children to research questions they identify as important. Children during this time read to learn and reach to achieve (Girl Scout Council of Cumberland Valley, 2001). Accommodating such a broad range of children's needs and abilities remains challenging for educators. The outdoor classroom provides viable formal and informal learning alternatives.

Children from ages 7 to 11 have short attention spans. They demonstrate present-time orientation with broad, often short-lived and unfocused, interests (Gilstrap et al., 1992). Thus, while children can be compelled to sit for long periods in drill and rote lessons, it is not conducive for their applied or long-term learning. Lessons providing children with both physical and mental mobility most effectively complement intellectual development. Activities allowing children to physically move about and interact with different materials and make choices regarding the learning process facilitate children's feelings of autonomy. Furthermore, by providing choices with respect to group membership and task responsibilities, children feel some control over their lives.

In order to develop initiative and follow-through, it is important to help children gain a positive self-concept. In doing so, they assume responsibility and develop perseverance because they feel a part of the decision-making process. Moving learning to the out-of-doors provides such an innovative venue for relevant learning. For some children, it is only in the out-of-doors, which offers greater mobility, flexibility, and interactions with community and other nonschool-related personnel, that they experience success. Task achievement and project involvement enhance self-esteem, which in turn facilitates responsibility and initiative.

Working With Curriculum

While state and local school districts provide curriculum guidelines, the ways in which educators achieve these objectives remains their instructional choice. When educators move school activities to the out-of-doors, the study is not necessarily limited to an aspect of the outdoor environment. Instead, the outdoors as classroom is perceived as a natural extension of the indoor classroom. The two environments work in tandem and support one another.

Planning a garden, constructing a pond, or observing weather patterns are typical outdoor activities. However, each involves indoor preparation before the outdoor activity can occur. The out-of-doors as classroom builds on the planning and follow-through of indoor learning.

The outdoors as classroom allows children to relate learning and their concrete stage abilities with relevant hands-on learning. The outdoor classroom allows children to practice numerous communication forms, rehearse a variety of social cueing criteria, and engage with diverse materials not available in the traditional classroom. Children's emerging sense of self benefits from myriad opportunities not possible from indoor pencil/paper learning. Extending interdisciplinary activities to the out-of-doors also facilitates academic achievement.

Projects

Project work is a way to connect with the out-of-doors and serves as a meaningful instructional alternative for active peer learning. For example, an investigation of the pathways surrounding the school involves children in measuring, interviewing, recording, and displaying information. Measuring the variety of pathways (driveways, sidewalks, nature trails, dirt and bike paths) surrounding the school affords children opportunities to use different kinds of measurement instruments and to perform a variety of calculations using authentic data. Interviewing school personnel regarding school pathways brings forth design, construction, and maintenance issues. For example, the students could inquire: "Who designed the school pathways and why was it done in this way?," "What do the design plans look like?," "Were there changes made from the original?," "Why?," "Who has input?," "Were there any disagreements?," "How do you bid for the construction of a school project?," "Who in the school is employed to maintain the pathways?," and "What equipment is used to build and maintain pathways?"

Through informal and formal discussions, children rehearse a variety of communica-

tion skills. Different interactions occur when children contact people other than the typical school-related personnel. The standards for social cueing and verbal/nonverbal communication invite different learning experiences. For example, students might need to find how to contact the original architect, and learn what is involved in conducting an interview. Allowing children to interact with nonschool-related adults provides them opportunities to develop and practice adult-like behaviors. In preparation, children ask, "How do I act?," "How do I dress?," "How should I take notes?," and "What information do I leave in a voice mail?" Finally, a broad project topic, like pathways, lends itself to numerous ways to collect information. In addition to traditional written text (learning logs, journals), children can use photographs, rubbings, sketches, maps, and audio/videotapes to collect and report findings (Chard, 1998). Children engage in learning tasks using both physical and mental effort. In doing so, it is possible to mediate a variety of learning styles and satisfy basic curriculum standards. Skills are practiced and mastered in a personally relevant context. When considering the out-of-doors as an extension for indoor lessons, relevant and authentic learning alternatives become abundant.

Clubs/Interest Groups/Sports

In addition to project work, helping elementary children to create clubs and special interest groups outside the classroom is a means of accommodating their emotional, social, and intellectual changes (Wiles & Bondi, 2001). Besides introducing children to a broad range of adults and adult-like activities, these clubs and interest groups also allow children a chance to mix with peers of different ages and genders (Wiles & Bondi, 2001). Positive peer interactions are important for children at this stage. Relating these organizations to the outdoors provides access to both community personnel and resources. Clubs represent children's diverse interests, from horses to cars, from trains to hot air balloons, and from archeology to gardening. Typical activities like biking, hiking, and Frisbee are attractive to elementary and adolescent children. In such clubs, children interact with committed and knowledgeable adults. Activities that involve children in sports also are popular at this age. In conjunction with competition and winning, sports activities can emphasize sportsmanship and cooperation. There are skills to be learned in both winning and losing.

When self-selected, these groups facilitate children's self-esteem. In turn, clubs and interest groups nurture children's responsibility and initiative. Finally, play at this age is also important. Wiles and Bondi (2001) indicate that because of fluctuations in basal metabolism, children can be listless at times and extremely restless at other times. They recommend ensuring opportunities for daily exercise and providing "a place where students can be children by playing and being noisy for short periods" (p. 34).

It is important to provide children at these ages with meaningful opportunities to interact with a broad range of school personnel (Wiles & Bondi, 2001). Providing children with innovative choices ensures they have opportunities to experience satisfaction and success. Extending clubs and groups to the out-of-doors allows children greater opportunity to build on their strengths and interests.

Success Through Out-of-Doors

Schools associated with successfully meeting student needs identify important aspects of their development, including: competence and achievement; self-exploration and definition; social interaction with peers and adults; physical activity; meaningful participation in school and community; routine, limits, and structure; and diversity (Lipsitz, 1984). Successful interactions with preadolescents also depend on opportunities to explore concepts, generate ideas from concrete experiences, and explore values and decision making (Johnston & de Perez, 1985). The outdoor classroom provides educators with numerous opportunities to highlight these components in ways not available in the indoor classroom.

The outdoor classroom provides children with innovative ways to accept responsibility in setting different standards for behavior than is possible in the traditional indoor classroom. Although children desire structure, they also question and reject suggestions (Wiles & Bondi, 2001). Plan-

Older children enjoy the freedom of the out-of-doors. Running is a favorite activity in all seasons.

ning ahead for outdoor activities provides a natural opportunity for children to be involved in setting the parameters for behavior. Children's mature value systems are facilitated when they engage different people with varied expectations. Finally, the outdoor classroom provides a unique aesthetic alternative. Experiencing the out-of-doors is not merely the means by which we pass from one indoor setting to another. Rather, the out-of-doors is to be appreciated in its own right.

Conclusion

Providing children consistent opportunities to engage in learning out-of-doors legitimizes the outdoor environment as an important place in their lives. Elementary-age children are not too old to go outside to learn and play. Yet children are spending less and less time outside. It may no longer be assumed that children have extended or natural opportunities to be out-of-doors. Educators have multiple opportunities to help children appreciate the potential of the out-of-doors by utilizing the outdoors as classroom. At the same time, educators will be providing relevant opportunities for children to mature socially, emotionally, and intellectually in ways not possible in the traditional indoor classroom.

References

Chard, S. C. (1998). *The project approach: Managing successful projects.* New York: Scholastic.

Gilstrap, R. L., Bierman, C., & McKnight, T. R. (1992). *Improving instruction in middle schools.* Bloomington, IN: Phi Delta Kappa Educational Foundation.

Girl Scouts of America, The. (2001). *Girl Scouts of Cumberland Valley.* Unpublished training manual provided to Girl Scout leaders.

Johnston, H. J., & de Perez, J. M. R. (1985). Four climates of effective middle schools. *Schools in the Middle, January,* 1-8.

Lipsitz, J. (1984). *Successful schools for young adolescents.* New Brunswick, NJ: Transactional Books.

McGlasson, M. (1973). *Middle school: Whence? What? Whither?* Bloomington, IN: Phi Delta Kappa Educational Foundation.

Shaffer, D. R. (1999). *Developmental psychology: Childhood and adolescence* (5th ed.). Pacific Grove, CA: Brooks/Cole Publishing.

Wiles, J., & Bondi, J. (2001). *The new American middle school: Educating preadolescents in an era of change.* Upper Saddle River, NJ: Merrill Prentice Hall.

CHAPTER 7

Deserted Playgrounds
The Importance of
Recess and Outdoor Play

Susan R. Van Patten

*Susan R. Van Patten is an Assistant Professor in the Department
of Recreation, Parks and Tourism at Radford University, Virginia.
Her background is in leisure behavior and recreation management,
with an emphasis in human interactions with the environment.*

School districts and state governments across the United States are responding to increasing demands for more academic success by curtailing or eliminating recess. This trend is worrisome, since recess is one of the primary opportunities children have to engage in social behavior with their peers, to practice such life skills as making friends and solving problems, and to have fun and exercise. It is estimated that nearly 40 percent of American elementary schools have removed recess completely from the school day, compared to only 10 percent in 1989 (Kieff, 2001; Pellegrini, 1995). Particularly threatened is the notion of "free time," when children can engage in unstructured, freely chosen activities. Instead, schools provide highly directed exercise activities through physical education. While supervision may be necessary at times, it is also important for children to make self-motivated choices.

Many administrators and school boards are being forced into eliminating recess by shrinking budgets, failing test scores, and state mandates requiring additional classroom hours. For example, Massachusetts passed new regulations in 1994 requiring elementary schools to provide 900 hours of structured learning time (an average of five hours a day), not including lunch, homeroom, breaks between classes, or recess ("Massachusetts' Student Learning," 1995). In 1996, Michigan increased instructional time to 990 hours, with an additional 15 percent increase forecasted for 2006 (Lee, 2001). Rather than extend the length of the school day or school year, recess and free time are squeezed out to accommodate these demands. What educators and parents must realize, however, is that increased instructional time does not necessarily lead to additional learning.

If the amount of instructional time were the primary correlate to academic success, then one would expect to see similar trends toward eliminating recess in countries that academically outperform the United States on a consistent basis. Yet this is not the case. In Great Britain, primary schools have three 15-minute recess periods plus an extended lunch break. Japan takes 10- to 20-minute breaks between 45-minute lessons and Taiwan incorporates multiple recess breaks into the school day (Jarrett et al., 1998). The primary difference in these countries is the amount of time children spend in school. Many of these countries have converted to year-round school or extended school weeks that include Saturday classes. While some American schools are abandoning the traditional nine-month school year with an extended summer break, many are holding onto the outdated agrarian calendar.

Fortunately, there is some hope for the future of recess. Besides outcries from some teachers, parents, and students lamenting the "death of fun" at school, some states finally are recognizing the necessity of recess. In 2000, the Virginia State Board of Education mandated that all elementary schools provide regularly scheduled recess as part of their instructional program (Virginia Beach City Public Schools, 2000). The benefits of outdoor play for children during recess are numerous and vital; as these benefits become clear, other states may take similar measures.

The Misunderstood Concept of Play

Perhaps the rapid decline of recess is due in part to our own ambivalence towards play, recreation, and leisure. Play is most closely associated with children's behavior, recreation through specific activities like sports, and free time away from work or other obligations. While these concepts often are used interchangeably, they actually have much deeper and complicated meaning and implications than appear on the surface.

Kraus (2001) defines play as:

A form of human or animal activity or behavioral style that is self-motivated and carried on for intrinsic, rather than external, purposes. It is generally pleasurable and is often marked by elements of competition, humor, creative exploration and problem solving, and mimicry or role playing. It appears most frequently in leisure activities, but may also be part of work. It is typically marked by freedom and lack of structure, but may involve rules and prescribed actions, as in sports and games. (p. 32)

Research indicates that play, in fact, may be an essential pursuit not only for children but also for adults. After all, humans are one of the few species that play as adults. An 80-year study following the lives of gifted children found that those individuals who had a more playful attitude tended to live longer (Terr, 1999). Anthropologist and play expert Garry Chick argues that play is an evolutionary trait valued in our pets as well as our mates (Marano, 1999). Chick argues that women may selectively choose mates who are willing to play, for their own protection as well as their children's.

Likewise, men view playfulness in women as an indicator of health and vitality.

While most adults recognize the inherent benefits of play, many distrust what they fear is frivolous behavior. The Protestant work ethic is contradictory to the notion of play, or what is perceived as wasted activity for pleasure. Thus, efforts to control children's play for educational and social purposes have been attempted since ancient Greek society. In medieval England, lawmakers went so far as to order boys to give up "dishonest and useless" games like ball games and dice in exchange for archery practice (Orme, 2001). Similar laws have been passed throughout history as societies attempt to manipulate children and adults into socially accepted forms of recreation and play. So-called "blue laws" are still on the books, dictating when and where we can engage in such disreputable activities as drinking, gambling, and even shopping.

Numerous theories explore children's need for play for the development of basic social and motor skills. Play deprivation theory postulates that when children are prevented from engaging in social and physical activities, a rebound or compensatory behavior will occur (Pellegrini, Huberty, & Jones, 1995). Deprived of such opportunities, children will become increasingly restless and distracted. Contrary to the argument that recess is detrimental to education, these findings indicate that recess may actually increase children's attention and academic performance.

Cognitive immaturity hypothesis reinforces that children have short attention spans and an innate desire to play, especially after periods of concentrated attention (Bjorklund & Green, 1992). Research indicates that children with recess are more focused and less distracted in class. A controlled experiment (Jarrett et al., 1998) with 43 fourth-grade children was conducted in an urban school system that did not usually have recess. Observations were made on behaviors related to concentration on work, fidgeting, and listlessness. On days when students did not have recess, students were on task 85 percent of the time and fidgeting 16 percent of the time. With recess, they were on task 90 percent of the time with only 7 percent fidgeting. Furthermore, all five of the children with attention deficit disorder (ADD) benefited from recess, spending more time on task and less time fidgeting, and seven of the 12 gifted children demonstrated marked improvement in at least one variable. Only six of the children seemed to be more distracted after recess, four of whom were from transient housing (no permanent home).

The ADD findings are especially important, considering the widespread use and abuse of Ritalin to control children's behavior. The Drug Enforcement Agency notes that Ritalin (methylphenidate), a drug prescribed primarily for ADD, produces effects similar to those of cocaine and amphetamines ("Methylphenidate," n.d.). Nearly one child in eight is taking Ritalin in the United States. In fact, the United States accounts for 85 percent of the world's Ritalin use even though it makes up only five percent of the global population (Sax, 2000). According to a study conducted in Maryland public schools, boys were four times more likely to be prescribed Ritalin and white children in general were prescribed Ritalin twice as often as their black and Hispanic counterparts (Safer & Malever, 2000). Children need to play; in the absence of play opportunities, U.S. society has turned to drugs to create passive children.

There are organizations fighting to ensure that children worldwide will be given the freedom to play. The International Association for the Child's Right to Play was founded in Denmark in 1961 to counter societies' indifference to the importance of play. The American branch of the Association for the Child's Right to Play emphasizes the following tenets (www.ipausa.org):

- Play is essential for the physical and mental health of the child
- Play is part of education
- Play is an essential part of family and community life
- Children need opportunities to play at leisure.

The needs of the child must have priority in the planning of human settlements. The issue of child's play has far-reaching consequences. While child labor is not a significant problem in the developed world, children in many countries still face bleak circumstances. In response to this issue, the General Assembly of the United Nations passed Article 31 of the UN Convention on the Rights of the Child on November 20, 1989 (www.ipaworld.org/ipa_article31). It states:

That every child has the right to rest, leisure and an opportunity to engage in play and recreational activities appropriate to the age of the child and to participate freely in cultural life and the arts. That member governments shall respect and promote the right of the child to participate fully in cultural and artistic life and shall encourage the provision of appropriate and equal opportunities for cultural, artistic, recreational and leisure activity.

Problems Facing Recess

Although many recognize that play is extremely important for children, schools must still be convinced that recess is the appropriate venue. Beyond simple time constraints during the school day, recess faces opposition from those teachers and parents who question the worthiness of setting time aside for children to "run wild." Part of this attitude goes back to the ambivalence toward play and leisure, but safety and social issues also are influential. With limited supervision, children face aggression and bullying from other students, the stigma of being left out, and potential injuries on playgrounds ("Is Recess Obsolete?," 1999). In Anne Arundel County, Maryland, none of the 30,000 grade school students have recess and the County Director claims that parents do not complain because it reduces injuries and fights ("Schools Taking Breaks," 2001). A nationwide survey of school principals found that more than a third claimed lawsuits and insurance problems had forced them to modify or eliminate recess ("No Time for Play," 2001).

Schoolyard violence is a growing problem, as demonstrated by a recent event in Chicago in which 19 children were injured and 23 students, ages 11 to 13, were charged with mob action when a rivalry between two elementary schools turned violent (Hepp & Olszewski, 2002). Safety issues, especially in outdoor settings, are commonly cited as a justification for removing recess from the curriculum, especially in poor and minority communities, which suffer from higher crime rates and inferior facilities (Kieff, 2001; Pellegrini, 1995).

Data suggest that ethnicity is a key factor in determining which schools will have recess. A study of Chicago public elementary schools found that schools with the highest percentage of poor and minority students were the least likely to have recess (Pardo, 1999). Recess is available in 50 percent of the schools with enrollment of at least 30 percent white students, compared to only 40 percent of those that are less than 5 percent white. The disparities are much more evident when comparing socioeconomic factors. Twelve of the 14 schools with less than 30 percent low-income students enjoy recess, compared to 10 percent of schools that serve predominantly low-income students. It should be recognized that recess decisions are not based upon race or poverty but rather academic performance, which is often lower in these groups. The consequences are the same regardless of the motivations.

Outdoor Play

While eliminating recess may provide a temporary fix to immediate problems facing schools, it may actually have a long-term negative effect. Recess traditionally occurs outside in some type of playground setting. Not only does outdoor play provide the greatest opportunities for novelty, it also tends to be more active, with fewer restrictions (Sawyers, 1994). This trend is even more pronounced for males, suggesting that outdoor play may be more necessary for boys (Pellegrini, 1991). However, some research shows that girls receive little or no encouragement to participate in physical activity during play periods (Sherman, 1998), which may partially explain these differences.

Providing opportunities for children to be active must become a high priority. According to the Centers for Disease Control and Prevention, the number of overweight children and teens has doubled in the last 20 years. Thirteen percent of children ages 6 to 11 years of age are overweight, and this number is only expected to increase ("More American Children," 2001). Significant weight gain can lead to such serious health problems as diabetes, high blood pressure, and heart disease. One of the primary contributing factors to weight gain is inactivity, which is exacerbated by the fact that 25 percent of children receive no physical education in school (Brody, 2000). This makes play time during recess even more necessary.

Great strides have been made in playground design to ensure safe and developmentally appropriate environments. Important considerations include the safety of equipment and materials, age-related activities, graduated challenges, and sufficient variety, complexity, and quantity of play spaces (Sawyers, 1994). Most important, supervision is critical to help guide children to appropriate activities and minimize conflicts.

When designing playscapes for children, attention also must be given to natural surroundings. International programs have been developed to incorporate environmental education into the curriculum. Schoolyard enhancement projects are currently underway in numerous states around the United States and in other countries. One such program is the Oxford-on-Rideau project, which is attempting to change a blandly landscaped area with little shade and few places to sit into a diverse setting for exploration and stimulation. Proposed enhancements include a tree grove, outdoor classroom, rock and mineral garden, bird and bat boxes, and a natural area ("Oxford-on-Rideau Schoolyard," n.d.). The National Wildlife Federation has promoted similar programs, with more than

2,180 certified schoolyard habitats in 2005 (www.nwf.org). Sweden has used the same philosophy to increase the number and variety of learning experiences by integrating natural aspects of the playground into the curriculum. Not only do these programs enrich students and teachers, they also help to eliminate much of the gender gap in outdoor play (Johnson, 1996).

Conclusions

Children cannot be expected to stay on task for extended periods of time. Therefore, eliminating opportunities for play in order to increase academic performance may cause more harm than good. To deny children the right to play is to deny them the opportunity to be children. Outdoor areas facilitate social and physical development, as well as environmental education. Many safety concerns about outdoor activities can be alleviated through proper playground design and appropriate supervision. Play is a right, not a privilege.

References

Bjorklund, D., & Green, B. (1992). The adaptive nature of cognitive immaturity. *American Psychologist, 47*, 46-54.

Brody, J. E. (2000, September 9). Fitness gap is America's recipe for fat youth. *The New York Times,* p. D8.

Hepp, R., & Olszewski, L. (2002, April 5). 19 kids hurt, 23 charged in elementary school brawl. *The Chicago Tribune* [Online], 30 paragraphs.

Is recess obsolete? (1999). *NEA Today, 17*(8), 43-45.

Jarrett, O. S., Maxwell, D. M., Dickerson, C., Hoge, P., Davies, G., & Yetley, A. (1998). Impact of recess on classroom behavior: Group effects and individual differences. *Journal of Educational Research, 92*(2), 121-128.

Johnson, J. E. (1996). Playland revisited: Growing is not necessarily for noses only. *Journal of Research in Childhood Education, 11*, 82-88.

Kieff, J. (2001). The silencing of recess bells. *Childhood Education, 77*, 319-321.

Kraus, R. (2001). *Recreation and leisure in modern society.* Boston: Jones and Bartlett.

Lee, A. (2001, June 1). Recess gets a makeover. *Detroit News* [Online], 20 paragraphs.

Marano, H. E. (1999). The power of play. *Psychology Today, 32*(4), 36-39.

Massachusetts' student learning time initiative.
(1995, July/August). *State Improvement Initiatives, 1*(6), 1-2.

Methylphenidate: Ritalin. (n.d.). Retrieved May 6, 2002, from www.usdoj.gov/dea/concem/ ritalin.htm

More American children and teens are overweight. (2001, March 12). Retrieved May 8, 2002, from www.cdc.gov/nccdphp/dnpa/press/archive/ overweight.htm

No time for play (2001, June 16). *The Economist,* p. 6.

Orme, N. (2001). Play in medieval England. *History, 51*(10), 49-55.

Oxford-on-Rideau schoolyard enhancement plan. (n.d.). Retrieved February 15, 2002, from www.ucdsb.on.ca/oxford/schoolyard/plan-schoolyardenhancement.html

Pardo, N. (1999, June). All work, less play in public schools. *Chicago Reporter* [Online], 80 paragraphs.

Pellegrini, A. D. (1991). Outdoor recess: Is it really necessary? *Principal, 70*(5), 40.

Pellegrini, A. D. (1995). *School recess and playground behavior: Educational and developmental roles.* Albany, NY: State University of New York.

Pellegrini, A. D., Huberty, P. D., & Jones, I. (1995). The effects of recess timing on children's playground and classroom behaviors. *American Educational Research Journal, 32*(4), 845-864.

Safer, D. J., & Malever, M. (2000). Stimulant treatment in Maryland public schools. *Pediatrics, 106*(3), 533-539.

Sawyers, J. K. (1994). The preschool playground: Developing skills through outdoor play. *Journal of Physical Education, Recreation & Dance, 65*(6), 31-33.

Sax, L. (2000, November). *Ritalin: Better living through chemistry? World and I.* Retrieved May, 6, 2002, from www.worldandi.com/public/2000/ November/sax.html

Schools taking breaks from recess. (2001, May 15). CNN.com, 29 paragraphs. Retrieved October 24, 2001, from wwwl1.cnn.com/2001/fyi/teachers/ ednews/05/15/recess.ap

Sherman, N. W. (1998). How physically active are students during recess periods? *Journal of Physical Education, Recreation & Dance, 69*(3), 11-12.

Terr, L. (1999). *Beyond love and work: Why adults need to play.* New York: Scribner.

Virginia Beach City Public Schools. (2000, August 24). *Questions and answers: Elementary school new recess guidelines.* Retrieved October 24, 2001, from www.vbcps.k12.va.us/recessga.html.

CHAPTER **8**

Swimming Upstream
Building a Case for Recess

Lynn A. Barnett

*Lynn A. Barnett is an Associate Professor in the Department of Recreation,
Sport and Tourism at the University of Illinois at Urbana-Champaign.
She focuses on the study of play, as it affords cognitive and emotional
benefits to the design of play settings, space, and materials.*

There are those who believe that participating in recess activities can be detrimental to children. These individuals typically buttress their argument by citing reports that decry the poor and declining performance of students across the United States, and the increasing differential in standardized achievement data compared with other nations. The recommendations from these reports often promote eliminating or severely restricting the nonacademic activities offered by school, since they are regarded as "nonessential" for the student's academic learning.

Still others suggest that the trend noted in declining test performance is not the result of an education system much in need of improvement, but rather that children are the unwitting victims of societal changes and upheaval. Proponents of this view cite statistics indicating that the "traditional" family of just a few decades ago is rapidly disappearing. The statistics on the growing divorce rate, and on the rise of single-parented families, two-parent working families, blended and step-families, with many transitions in between, all combine to affect the developing child. Children now have more to adapt to, and at younger ages, than was ever the case before. This pressure to adapt to and integrate a continually changing environment creates a great deal of stress, which is placed on ill-equipped children.

Much of the popular press has promulgated the notion that children today are more achievement-oriented and overprogrammed than they ever were. This generation of children is living in an increasingly achievement-oriented world, with standards and values that speak loudly to them that success is important (Eccles, Wigfield, & Schiefele, 1998). The notion that society has created the "Superkid" in response to changing demographics and these pressures to achieve has become popularized. Elkind's (2001) observations of children being "hurried" by these trends have been extended, as others recognize that the period of childhood is quickly disappearing (cf. Hymowitz, 2000; Postman, 1994). Schools mirror these societal trends: a school can be viewed as a small society in which its members must accomplish tasks, be socialized and socialize others, and be governed by rules that define and limit their behavior, feelings, and attitudes. This school society is now largely influenced by an increasingly demanding "cult of efficiency," which pushes the child to succeed and extols the value of hard work while devaluing the importance of play (Pellegrini & Bjorklund, 1996).

According to Elkind (2001), the harmful effects on the child of all of this pressure are pervasive: the self-perception of being a failure when skills are not easily learned or applied; the stress of constant transition and adaptation to several sets of milieus, rules, procedures, adult directions, and other children; the labeling of "hyperactive" or "learning disabled" when the new and rushed material is not readily digestible; the need to achieve becoming addictive; the perception that achievement is for the teacher and parent and is not intrinsically motivated; and the push to become more socially mature and responsible than is compatible with the child's age and maturational level. Elkind (2001) predicted that children who are under this type of stress would manifest its effects in several ways: feeling rejected as an individual because they are continually being shuffled from one arena to another; showing increased anxiety (restlessness, inability to concentrate, irritability, low mood); developing Type A behavior (competitive achievement striving, impatience, physical and verbal aggression); experiencing school burnout (emotional, psychological, and then, later, physical withdrawal from school); tending toward learned helplessness (expressing their inability to perform independently in a variety of school-related situations); assigning the motivation behind the child's activities to the adults; and then revolting by any one of several means (running away, getting involved with drugs, dropping out of school, becoming delinquent, or simply refusing to perform).

Elkind (2001) and others write that perhaps the biggest loss to the child as a result of these societal trends is the opportunity for free and undirected play. A recent comparison of how children spend their time in an average week found significant changes from 1981 to 1997. On average, children are in school over eight hours more per week than they were in the early 1980s, and they devote more than one hour additional time to studying. In contrast, the time they spend outdoors has decreased, with a sizeable reduction in the overall amount of play time each week (Institute for Social Research, 1997). Elkind (2001) argues that society has turned play into work for the child, and that this is a significant cause of the child's stress. His prescription for undoing the deleterious effects on the child is to allow significantly more periods of free and undirected play time.

Most authors who advocate for increased free-play time in the life of the child do so based on the wealth of evidence that documents the value of free play for individual development. They base their pronouncements on the literature, which indicates the important functions that play serves for the developing child (cf. Athey, 1984, 1988; Barnett, 1991; Bjorklund & Pellegrini, 2000; Curry & Bergen, 1988; Johnson, Christie, & Yawkey, 1999; King, 1987; Power, 2000; Rubin, Fein, & Vandenberg, 1983), and they reason that eliminating these opportunities will place the child at a distinct disadvantage in many important ways.

Prominent child development theorists have heralded the inherent value of free play to learning and development. Vygotsky (1978) believed play leads directly to the development of the child's conceptual abilities, enabling him/her to master abstract thought. Piaget's (1962) theory of child development positions play as a critical influence on the way in which the child comes to act on and adapt to his/her world. One of the underlying premises of Piaget's conceptualization is that children develop an understanding of their world when they are active and seek solutions for themselves. Children promote their own development when they actively engage with their environment. To build their knowledge, children need to be engaged in their learning on all fronts: physically, mentally, and emotionally. Children learn more by making their own discoveries and reflecting on them than by imitating adults or completing exercises to remember what they are told.

Thus, free play is of critical importance to the developing child, and few opportunities, apart from school recess, are left for children to engage in free play. A great deal of learning occurs in the "real life" world of the playground, much of which is not learned directly through classroom instruction but does affect the child's functioning in the classroom. Several characteristics set the classroom and recess worlds apart. One is that recess is a more "open" setting—a time when children are relatively free from adult intervention (other than limiting aggression) and when choices and the rules of engagement and interaction are much more their own. A second distinguishing characteristic reflects on the goals of children's play versus classroom environments. One of the central defining elements of play is that the means are more central and important than the ends; evaluation and judgments of outcomes by others are minimized, and consequences are less often promulgated. In school, however, the ends are more the focus of attention and reward, and scrutiny and evaluation are continuous and paramount. The ability to try things out in the absence of surveillance or judgment distinguishes play from more formalized classroom instruction, and designates it as a most inviting context for experimentation and active learning.

Children experience a wide spectrum of stresses in their lives, ranging from ordinary to severe (Melamed & Floyd, 1998). At the ordinary end are experiences that occur in most children's lives and for which they likely have reasonably well-defined coping patterns. Society also inflicts significant emotional stressors on children from a number of sources: pressing academic standards, family issues, and peer pressures. Many children who are forced to live in unsafe neighborhoods or chronic poverty, with burdensome responsibilities and economic uncertainties, experience considerable stress (Huston, 1995; Huston, McLoyd, & Coll, 1994; McLoyd, 1998; Sampson & Earls, 1995). Healthy coping patterns for these more stressful experiences are not as well-defined or readily accessible.

Many educators and parents have long noted the resemblance of children's themes in play and games to issues in their everyday world. Noted anthropologist Victor Turner (1982) wrote about the "human seriousness of play," noting how the content of play provides an introspective mirror into the child's reality. Freud (1955) also wrote extensively about the significance of play as a diagnostic medium through which adults can learn about the child's conflicts and trauma. His theory serves as the premise for play therapy, wherein clinical psychologists and court systems use play as an effective way of learning about and ameliorating traumatic events that have affected a child.

Over the years, children's games and rhymes have reflected the difficult realities in which children sometimes find themselves. Jump-rope rhymes and hand-clap games touch upon the themes of slavery, the Titanic, Hitler, and American patriotism (c.f. Abrahams, 1969; Bronner, 1988; Jones & Hawes, 1972; Knapp & Knapp, 1976; Newell, 1983; Opie & Opie, 1969; Schwartzman, 1978). Beresin (2002) recently detailed accounts of how children who were personally touched by the tragedy of September 11th used play to help allay their fears, thus allowing them to "move on." She observed a genre of games played by school children that mirrored the events and aftermath of the September 11 attacks, involving heroes, victims, frightened travelers, terrorists, panicked city dwellers, and children from schools that were closed. Based on these extensive observations, she concluded:

If September 11 has taught us anything, it is that . . . children's irrational play indeed makes a lot of sense. If we want to avoid what psychoanalysts call "trauma," we must allow children the opportunity to turn painful images into playful and artistic symbols for their release. Some need to play the attacker, some the attacked, some the shocked, some the defiant. Some need to recreate symbols, others to begin the search for new ones. . . . The seemingly trivial topic of play can be given more weight by its constant analysis and the dialogue it engenders. Play, in its brilliance, and trauma, in its heat, may be overlooked cultural illuminators. (Beresin, 2002, p. 335)

Research exploring the role of children's free-play opportunities in mitigating environmental stressors provides convincing evidence that play can help many children cope with traumatic events. The opportunity to "play through" a stressor neutralizes it and allows the child to assimilate the experience and make whatever adjustments are necessary in his/her own way. Laboratory and field investigations have supported the observations by Beresin (2002) and others, finding that children do indeed require free-play time to work through sources of anxiety (Barnett, 1982, 1984; Barnett & Storm, 1981; Gilmore, 1966). This line of research compared children who were anxiously upset by either contrived or naturally occurring stressors (hospital stays, pending surgeries, separation anxiety on the first day of school). In some of these studies, half of the children were allowed opportunities for free play, and the other half listened to a story read to them by a teacher. The findings were consistent: children used free play as a means of reducing their anxiety, and returned to their base line level of comfort following the free-play period. Following periods of free play, the children showed significantly lower measures of anxiety and distress compared to their cohorts who listened to a story, and they were equivalent to those who were not similarly anxious by these events. Barnett and Storm (1981) also examined what these anxious children did during their free play that effectively assuaged their anxiety, determining that the children employed many strategies and styles: some chose to interact with peers, some rebuffed overtures by others, and some elected to manipulate play materials related to the source of their anxiety. The authors concluded that children use play in a multitude of ways as an important means of dealing with distress. Thus, free play should be undirected and unstructured, to afford children maximal opportunity to gain the comforts they seek and in their own unique way. Sutton-Smith (1997) similarly argued, based upon theoretical writings and supporting evidence, that it is crucially important that play time be allowed and expanded during school time, especially during periods of undue stress and tragedy.

Coping skills among children vary widely; for example, one child may perceive an approaching test as threatening while another child may perceive it as challenging. What is stressful for a child depends on how s/he appraises and interprets the event (Lazarus, 1993). Even when children face adverse or stressful circumstances, certain characteristics buffer them against negative developmental outcomes and help make them resilient. Research indicates that some children are able to view environmental stressors more comfortably as chal-

lenges, and so triumph over some of life's adversities (Garmezy, 1985, 1993; Wilson & Gottman, 1996). The ability to acquire some measure of resilience during the middle school years, to be "stress-resistant" or even "invincible" (Garmezy, 1985; Werner & Smith, 1992), depends on a number of factors, many of which are developed and practiced during playful encounters with peers. During elementary school, a child who has several crucial strengths—particularly social and creative competencies—can help deflect or avoid many of the problems that may be encountered in the classroom, on the playground, at home, or in the community.

Goleman (1995) argued that when it comes to predicting a child's success in the world, and his/her ability to navigate life's travails, IQ matters less than the child's emotional intelligence. Emotional intelligence refers to the ability to understand and regulate emotions, to recognize and deal with one's own feelings and the feelings of others. This ability largely determines how well we use our mind and how we deal with "make-or-break" challenges, and it is largely set by adolescence. According to Goleman, several important aspects to emotional intelligence allow us to fare better in the world and successfully adapt to changing circumstances. One important component is the ability to use anxiety wisely. This means that we recognize that anxiety can serve a useful function, as long as it doesn't spin out of control and take us with it. Children can learn to use environmental stresses to their ultimate advantage—to develop problem-solving skills and learn to design strategies to successfully navigate through them.

Another of the components of emotional intelligence is the "people skills" readily recognized as empathy, and the ability to read a social situation. These skills help us to get along with others, successfully negotiate conflict and disagreement without resorting to violence, and make our social world work better for us and for others. Self-awareness is a crucial component of our emotional intellect because it allows us to learn and exercise self-control and to cope with rejection and discouragement. The idea is not to repress our natural feelings, but rather to become aware of them so that we can cope effectively with something troubling us. Such emotional learning is gained during a child's interactions with others, primarily peers, during recess and playground opportunities.

Consistent periods of free social play in recess are of crucial importance in developing and promoting this important type of emotional intellect. Many authors have proclaimed the playground during recess time as a significant "classroom for social interaction" (Pellegrini & Bjorklund, 1996). It provides unique opportunities for children to actively confront, interpret, and learn from meaningful social exchanges in their own way and at their own pace. The context of peer interaction on the playground is unique for learning social skills, in that the playful and non-serious tone allows children to experiment with, and refine, social strategies, most of which are not taught in the classroom. Pellegrini's influential work (1988, 1989a, 1989b) demonstrated the importance of recess as a time when elementary school children learn to solve social problems, resolve conflicts, negotiate, and work with others, particularly with minimal adult intervention. Pellegrini provided evidence that the recess behavior of the elementary school children he observed also related to their ability to solve hypothetical social problems, thus pointing to the more generalized effects of what is learned on the playground during recess.

Playground activities can draw children together, allowing them to develop and reinforce friendships. For some children, recess may serve as one of the few settings in which friendships can be formed and developed. Social knowledge is involved in children's ability to get along with their peers. Social relationship goals are important to them, such as how to initiate and maintain social bonds. The social world of children is made up of relationships of varying acquaintance. For several hours every day, they interact with some children they barely know and others with whom they have deeper friendships. Knowing how to develop and play out scripts that entice other children to be their friends is a major motivating force, and research indicates that this is a critically important undertaking. Friendships serve a number of significant functions in the child's life (Gottman & Parker, 1987; Hartup, 1996), and they shape children's emotional well-being and development (Sullivan, 1953). Hartup (1996; Hartup & Stevens, 1997) concluded that friendships foster self-esteem and provide a sense of confirmation and understanding, and they can be sources of significant cognitive and emotional support from childhood through old age.

Blatchford's (1998) recent work examining playground behaviors during school highlights the importance of recess in the development of friendships. From his longitudinal study of 7-, 11-, and 16-year-old children's experiences at recess, Blatchford concluded that recess provides an important context for children of all ages in the development of skills for fostering friendships and social relationships, and also in managing conflicts with peers. Blatchford demonstrated that friendships between children were consistently manifested in, and supported by, activities during recess and games on the playground. He concluded that friendship groups shared a common interest, purpose, and identity, and that this was particularly revealed and reinforced through interchanges that occurred at recess.

The playground is so widely regarded as a real-life laboratory for acquiring and developing social skills that many have advocated for its effective use in helping children of varying abilities with social development (e.g., McDermott, 1999; Thompson, Knudson, & Wilson, 1997). Children's relationships with their peers are fundamental to their mental health (Doll & Murphy 1996), and children who are rejected by their peers show the most serious long-term problems (Dishion & Li, 1996).

In addition to affording opportunities to construct social networks, develop and refine social skills, and build and reinforce friendships, recess allows children to get to know peers of different backgrounds and perspectives. An important dimension of the recess period is the opportunities it presents for a multitude of social interactions of varying type and intimacy. If one of the primary goals of education is to help children develop a democratic and inclusive orientation to society, then opportunities for social interactions with a diverse group of children in a relaxed and playful way are important.

Thus, children who have not adequately developed their social knowledge and skills through extended and varied social play opportunities are at a tremendous short- and long-term disadvantage. They are less likely to skillfully develop a significant part of their intellect, emotional functioning, and social relationships with peers and others. Children who have not utilized the opportunities offered by playground play to gain and refine their social knowledge are at an increasing risk for being marginalized by peers and adults and for, ultimately, threats to their developing self-concept and self-identity. In middle childhood, self-identity is formulated increasingly in reference to others, and these elementary social play experiences function in a critical way to provide feedback and self-affirmation.

Because recess is embedded in the school day, the question of its role in a child's education often arises (cf. Blatchford, 1998; Pellegrini, 1995; Pellegrini & Smith, 1998; Sutton-Smith, 1997). Most skeptics question the cognitive outcomes of children's play during recess. However, the literature amply documents the cognitive benefits of free play both in general (Barnett, 1991; Power, 2000; Rubin, Fein, & Vandenberg, 1983; Voss, 1987) and in the recess setting (for reviews, see Flaxman, 2000; Kieff, 2001; National Association of Early Childhood Specialists in State Departments of Education [NAECS/SDE], 2001; Pellegrini & Bjorklund, 1996; Pellegrini & Blatchford, 2000; Pellegrini & Smith, 1993; Tyler, 2000; Waite-Stupinsky & Findlay, 2001). Based on both theory and research, it is becoming increasingly recognized that to successfully perform in school, children must function in several realms. The cognitive arena is interrelated with the child's social and emotional functioning, and one arena should not be considered any less relevant or significant than the other. Thus, issues of emotional development and social competence must be considered as an important part of a child's education and performance. A wider definition of "education" must fully encompass the child's cognitive, social, and emotional development.

In conclusion, the contributions of experiences during recess play on the child's emotional and social development have received a great deal of recent empirical attention (for reviews, see Doll & Murphy, 1996; Jambor, 1994; McDermott, 1999; NAECS/SDE, 2001; Pellegrini & Bjorklund, 1996; Pellegrini & Blatchford, 2000; Sluckin, 1981; Smith, 1994; Towers, 1997; Tyler, 2000; Waite-Stupinsky & Findlay, 2001). The findings are reliable and provide justification to shareholders in the child's education that periods of free play should be consistently provided, and regarded as an integral and important part of the school day. Further, research findings dictate that the view of the playground as a classroom for social and emotional development be realized and adopted, perhaps equivalent in status to more structured and formal learning classroom opportunities. We must recognize that children use play as a way to work through difficult events in their lives, and learn about themselves and others through social relationships and negotiations, and that they should be allowed to do so in their own unique way. Adults should not dictate the type of activity or interaction that fills the recess period, and significant daily opportunities for free play should be provided.

References

Abrahams, R. (1969). *Jump rope rhymes: A dictionary.* Austin, TX: University of Texas Press.

Athey, I. (1984). Contributions of play to development. In T. D. Yawkey & A. D. Pellegrini (Eds.), *Child's play: Developmental and applied* (pp. 9-27). Hillsdale, NJ: Lawrence Erlbaum.

Athey, I. (1988). The relationship of play to cognitive, language, and moral development. In D. Bergen (Ed.), *Play as a medium for learning and development* (pp. 81-101). Portsmouth, NH:

Heinemann.

Barnett, L. A. (1982). Can pain be cured by play? *Parks and Recreation, 17*(4), 14-15.

Barnett, L. A. (1984). Young children's resolution of distress through play. *Journal of Child Psychology and Psychiatry, 25*(3), 477-483.

Barnett, L. A. (1991). The developmental benefits of play for children. In B. L. Driver, P. J. Brown, & G. L. Peterson (Eds.), *The benefits of leisure* (pp. 215-247). State College, PA: Venture Publishing.

Barnett, L. A., & Storm, B. (1981). Play, pleasure and pain: The reduction of anxiety through play. *Leisure Sciences, 4*(2), 161-176.

Beresin, A. R. (2002). Children's expressive culture in light of September 11, 2001. *Anthropology and Education Quarterly, 33*(3), 331-337.

Bjorklund, D. F., & Pellegrini, A. D. (2000). Child development and evolutionary psychology. *Child Development, 71*(6), 1687-1708.

Blatchford, P. (1998). *Social life in school: Pupils' experience of breaktime and recess from 7 to 16 years.* London: Falmer Press.

Bronner, S. (1988). *American children's folklore.* Little Rock, AR: August House.

Curry, N., & Bergen, D. (1988). The relationship of play to emotional, social, and gender/sex role development. In D. Bergen (Ed.), *Play as a medium for learning and development* (pp. 107-132). Portsmouth, NH: Heinemann.

Dishion, T. J., & Li, F. (1996, March). *Childhood peer rejection in the development of adolescent problem behavior.* Paper presented at the meeting of the Society for Research on Adolescence, Boston.

Doll, B., & Murphy, P. (1996, August). *Recess reports: Self-identification of students with friendship difficulties.* Paper presented at the annual meeting of the American Psychological Association, Toronto.

Eccles, J. S., Wigfield, A., & Schiefele, U. (1998). Motivation to succeed. In W. Damon (Ed.), *Handbook of child psychology* (5th ed., Vol. 3, pp. 1017-1095). New York: Wiley.

Elkind, D. (2001). *The hurried child: Growing up too fast, too soon* (3rd ed.). Cambridge, MA: Perseus.

Flaxman, S. G. (2000). Play: An endangered species. *Instructor, 110*(2), 39-41.

Freud, S. (1955). Beyond the pleasure principle. In J. Strachey (Ed.), *The standard edition of the complete psychological works of Sigmund Freud* (Vol. XVIII, pp. 7-64). London: Hogarth.

Garmezy, N. (1985). Stress-resistant children: The search for protective factors. In J. E. Stevenson (Ed.), *Recent research in developmental psychopathology* (pp. 213-233). New York: Pergamon Press.

Garmezy, N. (1993). Children in poverty: Resilience despite risk. *Psychiatry, 56*, 127-136.

Gilmore, J. B. (1966). Play: A special behavior. In R. N. Haber (Ed.), *Current research in motivation* (pp. 334-355). New York: Holt, Rinehart & Winston.

Goleman, D. (1995). *Emotional intelligence.* New York: Bantam.

Gottman, J. M., & Parker, J. G. (1987). *Conversations of friends.* New York: Cambridge University Press.

Hartup, W. W. (1996). The company they keep: Friendships and their developmental significance. *Child Development, 67*, 1-13.

Hartup, W. W., & Stevens, N. (1997). Friendships and adaptation in the life course. *Psychological Bulletin, 121*, 355-370.

Huston, A. C. (1995, August). *Children in poverty and public policy.* Paper presented at the meeting of the American Psychological Association, New York City.

Huston, A. C., McLoyd, V. C., & Coll, C. G. (1994). Children and poverty: Issues in contemporary research. *Child Development, 65*, 275-282.

Hymowitz, K. S. (2000). *Ready or not: What happens when we treat children as small adults.* San Francisco: Encounter Books.

Institute for Social Research. (1997). *Healthy environments, healthy children. Child development supplement: Panel study of income dynamics.* Ann Arbor, MI: University of Michigan Institute for Social Research.

Jambor, T. (1994). School recess and social development. *Dimensions of Early Childhood, 23*(1), 17-20.

Johnson, J. E., Christie, J. F., & Yawkey, T. D. (1999). *Play and early childhood development* (2nd ed.). New York: Longman.

Jones, B., & Hawes, B. L. (1972). *Step it down: Games, plays, songs and stories from the Afro-American heritage.* Athens, GA: University of Georgia Press.

Kieff, J. (2001). The silencing of recess bells. *Childhood Education, 77*, 319-320.

King, N. R. (1987). Elementary school play: Theory and research. In J. H. Block & N. R. King (Eds.), *School play: A source book.* New York: Garland.

Knapp, N., & Knapp, H. (1976). *One potato, two potato: The folklore of American children.* New York: W. W. Norton.

Lazarus, R. S. (1993). Coping theory and research. *Psychosomatic Medicine, 55*, 234-247.

McDermott, K. (1999). Helping primary children work things out during recess. *Young Children, 54*(4), 82-84.

McLoyd, V. C. (1998). Children in poverty. In W. Damon (Ed.), *Handbook of child psychology* (5th ed., Vol. 4, pp. 135-208). New York: Wiley.

Melamed, B. G., & Floyd, B. (1998). Childhood stress. In H. S. Friedman (Ed.), *Encyclopedia of Mental Health* (Vol. 1, pp. 409-420). San Diego, CA: Academic Press.

National Association of Early Childhood Specialists in State Departments of Education (NAECS/SDE). (2001). *Recess and the importance of play: A position statement on young children and recess.* Denver, CO: NAECS/SDE Center for At-Risk Education.

Newell, W. W. (1983). *Games and songs of American children.* New York: Dover.

Opie, I., & Opie, P. (1969). *Children's games in streets and playgrounds.* London: Clarendon.

Pellegrini, A. D. (1988). Elementary-school children's rough-and-tumble play and social competence. *Developmental Psychology, 24*(6), 802-806.

Pellegrini, A. D. (1989a). Elementary school children's rough-and-tumble play. *Early Childhood Research Quarterly, 4*, 245-260.

Pellegrini, A. D. (1989b). What is a category? The case of rough-and-tumble play. *Ethology and Sociobiology, 10*, 331-341.

Pellegrini, A. D. (1995). *School recess and playground behavior: Educational and developmental roles.* Ithaca, NY: SUNY Press.

Pellegrini, A. D., & Bjorklund, D. F. (1996). The place of recess in school: Issues in the role of recess in children's education and development. *Journal of Research in Childhood Education, 11*, 5-13.

Pellegrini, A. D., & Blatchford, P. (2000). *The child at school: Interactions with peers and teachers.* New York: Oxford University Press.

Pellegrini, A. D., & Smith, P. K. (1993). School recess: Implications for education and development. *Review of Educational Research, 63*(1), 51-67.

Pellegrini, A. D., & Smith, P. K. (1998). Physical activity play: The nature and function of a neglected aspect of play. *Child Development, 69*(3), 577-598.

Piaget, J. (1962). *Play, dreams, and imitation in childhood.* New York: W.W. Norton.

Postman, N. (1994). *The disappearance of childhood.* New York: Vintage Books.

Power, T. G. (2000). *Play and exploration in children and animals.* Mahwah, NJ: Lawrence Erlbaum.

Rubin, K. H., Fein, G. G., & Vandenberg, B. (1983). Play. In P. H. Mussen (Ed.), *Handbook of child psychology* (4th ed., Vol. 4, pp. 693-774). New York: Wiley.

Sampson, R. J., & Earls, F. (1995, March). *Community social organization in the urban mosaic: Project on human development in Chicago neighborhoods.* Paper presented at the meeting of the Society for Research in Child Development, Indianapolis, IN.

Schwartzman, H. (1978). *Transformations: The anthropology of children's play.* New York: Plenum.

Sluckin, A. (1981). *Growing up on the playground: The social development of children.* London: Routledge and Kegan Paul.

Smith, P. K. (1994). What children learn from playtime, and what adults can learn from it. In P. Blatchford & S. Sharp (Eds.), *Breaktime and the school: Understanding and changing playground behavior* (pp. 36-48). London: Routledge.

Sullivan, H. S. (1953). *The interpersonal theory of psychiatry.* New York: W.W. Norton.

Sutton-Smith, B. (1997). *The ambiguity of play.* Cambridge, MA: Harvard University Press.

Thompson, S., Knudson, P., & Wilson, D. (1997). Helping primary children with recess play: A social curriculum. *Young Children, 52*(6), 17-21.

Towers, J. (1997). The neglect of playtime: A review of the literature. *Early Child Development & Care, 131*, 31-43.

Turner, V. (1982). *From ritual to theatre: The human seriousness of play.* New York: Performing Arts Journal Publications.

Tyler, V. (2000). Why recess? *Dimensions of Early Childhood, 28*(4), 21-23.

Voss, H-G. (1987). Exploration and play: Research and perspectives in developmental psychology. In D. Gorlitz & J. F. Wohlwill (Eds.), *Curiosity, imagination and play: On the development of spontaneous cognitive and motivational processes* (pp. 44-58). Hillsdale, NJ: Lawrence Erlbaum.

Vygotsky, L. S. (1978). *Mind in society.* Cambridge, MA: Harvard University Press.

Waite-Stupinsky, S., & Findlay, M. (2001). The fourth R: Recess and its link to learning. *Educational Forum, 66*(1), 16-25.

Werner, E. E., & Smith, R. S. (1992). *Vulnerable but invincible: A longitudinal study of resilient children and youth.* New York: McGraw-Hill.

Wilson, B. J., & Gottman, J. M. (1996). Attention—the shuttle between emotion and cognition: Risk, resiliency, and physiological bases. In E. M. Hetherington & E. A. Blechman (Eds.), *Stress, coping, and resilience in children and families* (pp. 189-228). Hillsdale, NJ: Lawrence Erlbaum.

CHAPTER 9

The Value of Play as a Developmental Mechanism in Pre- and Early Adolescence

Chip Wood

Chip Wood, M.S.W., is Principal of Sheffield Elementary School in Turners Falls, Massachusetts. He is author of books and articles on education and is a co-founder of the Responsive Classroom® approach to professional development.

The phrase "cooking the books" refers to the actions of corporations that falsely inflate the value of their companies by hiding enormous expenses. These scandals, which continue to ripple through the financial world, with ethical and social consequences on society, have a parallel in the field of public education. Schooling today should be criticized for "cooking the kids" without accounting for the hidden expenses. "Cooking the kids" refers to the increasing expenditure of time on standardized tests as the single visible measure of learning, supposedly translating into "educational profitability."

Cooking the Kids

While seeking to "leave no child behind," the education establishment and federal government systematically leave childhood behind for millions of school-age children. More time spent on direct instruction, test preparation, test taking, and test review results in less time for learning, creativity, physical activity, and play. More than 40 percent of elementary schools in the United States have eliminated one or more recess periods from children's school day (Ohanian, 2002). Accountability in education, as in business, is defined as growth in profits. The profits are not measured by the progress of the children themselves, however, but by the test scores. While no one argues with the need to improve children's academic skills, this goal cannot be reached at the expense of undermining children's physical, social, and emotional development. These are the hidden costs of the attempt to raise the academic bar. In the late 1970s, a similar "pushed down" curriculum and "back to basics" trend eventually gave way to the "push back" movement, guiding instruction toward more developmentally appropriate practices (as espoused by the National Association for the Education of Young Children [NAEYC]). With today's emphasis on standardized test scores, the education pendulum is once more returning to a "basic skills" or "direct instruction" approach. Children are increasingly being asked to master academic skills and spend more time on academic tasks at younger ages.

In the rush for academic achievement, developmental needs for 8- to 12-year-old children are being thwarted. Fortunately, teachers, administrators, parents, nurses, pediatricians, and child development experts are speaking out with increasing urgency and outrage against the inappropriate curriculum, homework, and scheduling of children's time in and out of school (Ohanian, 2002; Orlich, 2000). This growing concern derives from knowledge about children's learning and development. One way to protect development is to provide quality play experiences and opportunities for children ages 8 through 12 years old. In particular, the outdoors provides these children with unique opportunities not available in the traditional indoor classroom.

Play As Foundation to Development

Child development experts know that play is foundational and essential to cognitive growth in social, moral, and academic understanding. Play also is significant to basic identity formation. Generally, play is sanctioned only at home, preschool, and in the early elementary grades. From ages 8 through 12, children's social interactions are being seriously limited and, therefore, their development is jeopardized. The consequences of limited time and opportunity for children to socially interact includes less opportunity for affective traits to inform the identity of the emerging person. This is no small matter in the development of character, social cognition, and morality. As Haviland and Kahlbaugh (1993) argue, "An *adaptive* and *recognizable* identity would be interconnected with sets of rules that offer useful information about life and that are emotionally dense" [emphases added] (p. 328).

These interconnections, as Piaget noted, often are made when children are at play, right through the teenage years. As Haviland and Kahlbaugh further indicate, "Identity is the ordered sum of relationship skills, cognitive skills, feelings, physical abilities, and so forth. These traits are associated with the roles one performs, including relationship roles, work roles and cultural roles, producing an amalgamated identity or self-structure" (p. 333). The roles that children (including older children) are drawn to and "perform" are play roles occurring during spontaneous free play, recess, and after-school activities. This role rehearsal even appears in structured athletics (inventing games within game structures).

In the scheme of growing up, learning through play occurs quite naturally, because children have been given the protection of a protracted period of development in which they unmistakably experience life playfully in the present. By eliminating or curtailing play for pre-adolescents and young adolescents, and replacing it with an adult model of work, we take a great risk of deforming childhood and adolescence. We see that the rate of childhood and teenage depression, and the use of psychopharmacology to control mood and behavior, particularly in school settings, has increased each year (DeGrandpre, 1999).

Children and Time

Children live in real time—a natural world of time, which knows only the present moment—long before they can tell time. Think back to memories of childhood, when you were lost in time at the edge of the ocean building sandcastles or when playing with imaginary friends. The grace of these present moments recedes as time becomes bracketed, contextualized, by past and future.

Poet Billy Collins (1995), captures what happens as we become more aware.

ON TURNING TEN

The whole idea of it makes me feel
like I'm coming down with something,
something worse than any stomach ache
or the headaches I get from reading in bad
*   light—*
a kind of measles of the spirit,
a mumps of the psyche,
a disfiguring chicken pox of the soul.

You tell me it is too early to be looking back,
but that is because you have forgotten
the perfect simplicity of being one
and the beautiful complexity introduced by
*   two.*
But I can lie on my bed and remember
*   every digit.*
At four I was an Arabian wizard.
I could make myself invisible
by drinking a glass of milk a certain way.
At seven I was a soldier, at nine a prince.

But now I am mostly at the window
watching the late afternoon light.
Back then it never fell so solemnly
against the side of my tree house,
and my bicycle never leaned against the
*   garage*
as it does today,
all the dark blue speed drained out of it.
This is the beginning of sadness, I say to

myself,
as I walk through the universe in my
*   sneakers.*
It is time to say good-bye to my imaginary
*   friends,*
time to turn the first big number.

It seems only yesterday I used to believe
there was nothing under my skin but light.
If you cut me I could shine.
But now when I fall upon the sidewalks of
*   life,*
I skin my knees, I bleed.

Piaget was first to recognize the complexity of time concepts in the developing mind of the child. In *The Child's Conception of Time* (1927), he made clear that children do not perceive time the same way adults do, and by helping us understand that their early conceptions of time explain certain behaviors.

As children grow beyond preschool and primary years, they begin to develop an understanding of present, past, and future—of what is called "diachronic thinking." "Diachronic thinking" refers to children's developing ability to show their understanding of transformations across time, such as the growth of living things and changes in the weather. Children utilizing a diachronic approach in their thinking exhibit "a type of attitude or tendency of thought that consists of the spontaneous comparison of a current situation with its past and future states" (Montangero, 1996, p. 80), the same perspective reflected in Collins's poem.

This "tendency of thought" develops across time. By 8 or 9 years of age, children have a better sense of duration and comparative durations because they are now able to "conserve" concepts, holding onto more than one idea at the same time. They can conceive of reforestation without human intervention, and struggle with classic math problems.

At 11 or 12 years of age, a cognitive leap occurs in children's diachronic thinking and approaches to problem solving. This coincides with growth in other cognitive processes, such as more abstract reasoning, even about concrete problems. All this change seems to be the cumulative growth of cognition.

Older elementary children can see changes over time as successive states within an evolutionary process, such as trees growing, ice thawing, or knowledge evolving. "This new perspective allows children to enrich their evocations and explanations by the use of concepts such as cycles, evolutions, transmission from one generation to the next, etc. to which they previously had only recognitive access" (Montangero, 1996, p. 181). Although younger children may recognize the words that indicate changes across an extended time (such as "evolution" or "reforestation"), they cannot easily grasp the concepts denoted by the words. Eight- through 12-year-old children at play, especially fantasy play associated with time travel, however, can experience a cognitive co-mingling of their experience with fiction and their developing understanding of history, geography, and science into new conceptual constructions. This will not take place as richly or deeply through solitary reading (Wood, 2000).

Play among 8- through 12-year-olds provides a meaningful arena for cognitive construction involving the imagination, rule generation, physical prowess, probability, artistic expression, and group problem solving within an emerging diachronic understanding of life experience. When the arenas of life for 8- to 12-year-olds are increasingly limited to teacher-directed instruction, recall and test taking, homework completion, television and video games, and adult, rule-bound extracurricular activities and sports, the depth and context of identity formation is compromised.

What Does Play Provide for the Elementary Years?

Play is rehearsal for all manner of activity for children in 2nd through 6th grades. Dramatic play in the classroom can rehearse writing. Role-playing can rehearse social problem solving. Play is proactive. It is practice. It honors invention and reinvention through its pretend and transitory nature. It values mistakes and revision, all so important to solving math problems, experimenting in science, and drafting a poem. It is no wonder that myriad board games and card games have been created for children at these ages as they explore the rules, structures, and social nuances of play.

The out-of-doors provides older children with unique opportunities to engage their peers during play.

During play, time stands still. Games create an environment, a container of play and child-sized reality that feels both emotionally "dense" and usually safe (even though there will be arguing).

Traditionally, outdoor play at recess or in neighborhoods has served as rehearsal for friendship between older children and as initial markers of interest in members of the opposite gender. Whether in the highly physical chase games involving gangs of girls and boys moving in waves across the playground at 8 years of age or the more sophisticated chasing in Capture-the-Flag, Red Rover, or Four Corners in older grades, there is as much talking, laughing, arguing, and shouting as there is running. Picking sides, changing the rules, and deciding who won are all important to children at this age. These are ways children exchange social capital and learn about each other. Where will they be able to exchange this social capital if recess is replaced with more structured sports activity on the playground? The consequences of eliminating recess and limiting children's play opportunities may be seen today in discipline problems and children's aggression.

The oft-quoted phrase "play is a child's work" generally refers to toddler and preschool play, yet it is also true of older children. Play is work for older children as they gather and trade their collections of rocks, stickers, baseball cards, and the unending fad items that come and go on the social capital market of the playground, classroom, and home marketplace. Play is work as it becomes more and more competitive and stratified, and as children come to repeatedly experience that talent, skill, practice, culture, class, and popularity are all serious business on the playing field. Older children also play at strife, which sometimes becomes their labor. Cliques form and reform in the games of relationships (Simmons, 2002).

The transition of play as work to work as play can occur during this age span for those children fortunate enough to have ongoing positive experiences with cooperative and collaborative academic endeavors, service learning projects, and experiential learning activities, including skillful play initiatives, cooperative games, and camping experiences. These all provide older children with validation and reinforcement for such behaviors as guessing, hypothesizing, reasonable risk taking, calculated experimentation, revision, perseverance, and reflection—all within the context of clear, rule-bound peer social interaction under expert adult facilitation and supervision. Schoolwork, community service work, or even homework can be valued and validated equally for the accomplishment of a community of peers at play. Individual achievement of any one member is assessed within the group endeavor. Even in communities or schools where older children experience these activities only a portion of the time, they are at least provided with a comparative experience of the purpose of work, the work process, and the affective influences of work for their lives.

Reflection as Play

As 8- through 12-year-old children become more capable of abstract thinking, including the ability to take perspective, time for reflection in their lives becomes essential. This is a largely missing ingredient in today's developmental recipe for character and identity formation. Parents, teachers, and coaches must ensure time is available for reflection. And children need and seek reflection with strong, adult role models who can act as skillful listeners.

Preadolescent and young adolescent children need time for solitary reflection to begin the adolescent journey of discovering who they are. Daydreaming is a critical play activity of the older child and seldom a waste of time. It provides respite and healing from the "rapid-fire culture" that demands so much of older children's intellect and emotions and does so little to feed their souls (DeGrandpre, 1999). The out-of-doors provides a myriad of unique opportunities for solitary reflection. Outdoor walking near trees or water, skipping stones on a small lake, shooting hoops or throwing a ball against a back wall—these activities allow children to utilize the physical exertion often necessary for mental introspection. Sometimes, outdoor reading, sketching, painting, or journaling allows children to satisfy some quiet thoughts or sparks some potential expression. Such opportunities deepen the experiences of children and refresh their spirit to promote their achieving quality in their lives.

Children also need time for reflection with peers. On the playground and playing field it can be as simple as circling up (after shaking hands with the other team) at the end of a contest to thank teammates, note an opponent's worthiness, or make a suggestion for the next game. The out-of-doors holds the potential to shape children's lives in different ways and gives them strategies for the hard and beautiful times ahead.

Can we doubt the multi-layered significance of play in the lives of children in the middle of their childhood? The out-of-doors provides natural opportunities for children to engage in introspection and also to apply their emerging social abilities and interpret the actions of others. The out-of-doors provides a plethora of opportunities and activities to engage and enrich the development of the 8- through 12-year-old child.

References

Collins, B. (1995). *The art of drowning*. Pittsburgh, PA: University of Pittsburgh Press. (with permission)

DeGrandpre, R. (1999). *Ritalin nation: Rapid-fire culture and the transformation of human consciousness*. New York: W.W. Norton & Co.

Haviland, J. M., & Kahlbaugh, P. (1993). Emotion and identity. In M. Lewis & J. M. Haviland (Eds.), *Handbook of emotions* (pp. 327-340). New York: The Guilford Press.

Montangero, J. (1996). *Understanding changes in time*. Bristol, PA: Taylor and Francis.

Ohanian, S. (2002). *What happened to recess and why are our children struggling in kindergarten?* New York: McGraw Hill.

Orlich, D. C. (2000, February). Education reform and limits to student achievement. *Phi Delta Kappan, 83*(6), 468-472.

Piaget, J. (1927). *The child's conception of time*. New York: Basic Books,

Simmons, R. (2002). *Odd girl out: The hidden culture of aggression in girls*. New York: Harcourt Books.

Wood, R. (2000). *Time to teach, time to learn: Changing the pace of school*. Greenfield, MA: North East Foundation for Children.

CHAPTER 10

Rough and Tumble Play
An Integral Part of Growing Up

Tom Reed and Mac Brown

Tom Reed is an Associate Professor of Early Childhood Education at the University of South Carolina Upstate. He is an active member of the International Play Association (IPA) and the Association for the Study of Play (ASP). Mac Brown is a Professor of Early Childhood Education at the University of South Carolina Columbia. He provided a leadership role in the creation of the new public-private U.S.C./Gateway Child Development and Research Center.

Play has never been universally defined in the literature. Perhaps no simple definition can be determined, as there are as many different interpretations of play as there are cultures in the world. Csikszentmihalyi (1975) suggests that play is supposed to be fun and something to be "felt," not necessarily "done." This chapter focuses on a specialized type of play, referred to as rough and tumble play (R&T), that is rooted in pedagogical theory. Constructivist theory proposes that R&T begins in the preoperational stage and continues into concrete operations, following a predictable developmental path (Piaget & Inhelder, 1969). From this perspective, R&T combines both physiological and experiential abilities, and precedes games with rules. The constructivist approach theory stresses that play functions to create symbols and schemas needed for an idiosyncratic view of the world. Therefore, R&T is a function of culture and learned behavior necessary for membership (Cole, John-Steiner, Scribner, & Souberman, 1978).

Rough and tumble play was brought to popular notice by Harlow's (1962) research with Rhesus monkeys. Harlow described the basic tenets of R&T as running, chasing and fleeing, wrestling, open-hand slap, falling, and play fighting. Children routinely chase one another with no intent to capture their quarry. Those who engage in wrestling as part of R&T do not intend to hurt their partners. There is much slapping or pushing in R&T that remains playful; yet, there may be feigning of injury. In addition to all of these socially driven and playful, yet somewhat aggressive, behaviors that Harlow described is the play face. Harlow describes the play face as an opened-mouth, teeth-bared expression, which looks fierce but actually denotes that the intent is non-aggressive and playful. Children use this same play face frequently, accompanied by smiles and laughter, to communicate that their rough behavior is R&T and not true aggression.

The Affective Domain

Rough and tumble play is pervasive in western culture and has been institutionalized or ritualized in major spectator events such as soccer, football, basketball, hockey, and stock car racing etc. R&T behaviors have become institutionalized in such time-honored games as Kickball, King of the Mountain, Red Rover, and the classic "I'm Gonna Get You/You Can't Catch Me" game played with toddlers (Sutton-Smith, 1992). In addition to having fun, children who participate in R&T benefit in other ways. Pellegrini (1994) clearly establishes that engagement in R&T is positively correlated with social problem-solving ability and academic achievement among boys. Social competence is developed through alternating role-taking, give-and-take, deciding who is to follow and who is to lead, and exploring social dominance. Furthermore, academic achievement is related to social adjustment and competence in problem solving, which are both refined during R&T (Pellegrini, 1994).

Noddings (1992) describes "to care" and "to be cared for" as basic human needs. Caring does not adhere to a prescribed formula. This makes it difficult for schools to help children learn to care for other human beings. Gender- and culture-based considerations affect teaching children to care. Gender-specific methods of caring must be considered, because it is apparent that boys and girls have different perspectives on intimate relations and different interpretations with regard to connection and expression of care (Noddings, 1992). Elementary schools are often governed by the feminine perspective, which considers pushing, hitting, shoving, or games of chase and flee (factors common to R&T) as inappropriate behaviors.

All physical activity is inherently risky (Fagen, 1981). Women are more likely to view R&T as aggressive, while men are likely to see it as play (Conner, 1989). R&T has the appearance of being aggressive, which may be part of its appeal to young boys. Play theorists have attempted to explain the difference between R&T and aggression. The uninformed observer of R&T may see the tripping, pushing, or hitting as fighting; indeed, one definition of R&T is play fighting (Blurton-Jones, 1976). Donaldson (1976) theorizes that what is actually occurring is hugging, loving, compassion, embracing, mutual sharing, and concern for one another masked as aggression. He states that the R&T player is saying, "I trust you to push me, trip me, fall on me, and if I get hurt you will care for me" (Donaldson, 1976, p. 239). Research has documented that R&T is a distinct category of behavior separated from aggression (Blurton Jones, 1976; Sutton-Smith, 1992). Pellegrini (1989) found that R&T breaks down into aggression in less than 3 percent of all cases and represents less than 11 percent of all playground activity.

Merriam-Webster's Collegiate Dictio-

nary (1994) defines a "friend" as "one attached to another by affection or esteem" (p. 467). The *Oxford American Dictionary* (1999) further defines friendship as a relationship. Other definitions of friendship include such characteristics as intimate, mutually supportive, voluntary reciprocal, sacrificing, and rewarding (Kochender & Ladd, 1996). Ginsberg, Gottman, and Parker (1986) found essential ingredients of friendships to include intimacy, affection, and ego support. Many researchers agree that the concept of friendship itself is a social construct that involves reaching a shared meaning, and that it does not necessarily come naturally (Bukowski, Newcomb, & Hartup, 1996; Burk, 1996; Lawhon, 1997). The arena in which children choose to build this knowledge is play that enhances social skills and leads to stable friendships (Lawhon, 1997).

Introduction to Our Project

The following project examined the way in which primary school-age boys engage in R&T, and described their interactions and relationships with each other in their natural surroundings. The criteria for recognizing and recording an episode of R&T included reciprocal role-taking, the play face, vigorous movement, and alternating between victim and victimizer (Pellegrini, 1995). Participants were involved in two individual interviews plus one final group interview. Observations were conducted in a youth center for school-age children within a United States Air Force military installation located in the southeastern United States. The student population of the youth center was composed from diverse socioeconomic backgrounds, and Asian, black, Hispanic, and white children attended.

In all, 119 demonstrations of R&T were observed, taped, and analyzed. Selected episodes of R&T were viewed and discussed with the participants by the authors. Sixty of the R&T episodes were observed during a game following the "tackle the boy with the ball" format referred to by the participants as "Smear the Queer." It should be noted that despite the repugnant nature of the name Smear the Queer (hereafter referred to as "Smear"), the players coined the term and it was not used in any other context. An examination of the findings clearly indicate that R&T is indeed a means by which boys express care and intimacy for one another. Seventy-three demonstrations of caring and intimate contact were observed during the 119 episodes of R&T. In addition, these findings indicate that all R&T episodes, except those involving non-playing intruders, occur within the context of friendships and caring relationships. The following findings were commonalities that emerged from the observations:

- R&T provides the opportunity for the declaration of friendship and caring relations
- R&T involves intimate contact that is met with understanding by the players
- R&T resembles a ritualized type of play that requires specific knowledge
- All of the regular R&T players knew or observed the rules
- Knowledge of rules separated R&T players from intruders
- R&T resulted in one minor injury.

R&T Is a Declaration of Friendship and Caring

In choosing to play the game of Smear, the seven participants were declaring their friendship. They felt that R&T gave them an opportunity to show that they cared for each other. The aggressive nature of Smear (which is very much like American football) is part of what draws the players to it. The players enjoyed playing Smear because they got to be with their friends and, quite frankly, they liked to be tackled. Most of the players are friends, but one boy pointed out that "Some aren't. It doesn't really matter. We are having fun." It appears that friendship was considered by the participants to be a prerequisite for participating in R&T. Several of the tackles during Smear resulted in a pile of bodies on top of one another, which often resulted in checking to see if the fallen were hurt.

When asked why they wanted to check on each other so much, one player thought for a moment and said, "Well, we're best friends" and "We're like brothers." In summary, R&T appears to be the vehicle by which friendships are nurtured.

R&T Involves Intimate Physical Contact

The participants of R&T seemed to display a healthy respect for personal boundaries, which was expressed through physical contact that, at times, was quite intimate. While the participants knew what was considered appropriate touch during R&T, they were less certain outside of the play arena. This lack of certainty was shown in responses to questions regarding whether it was appropriate to touch when outside the realm of R&T and, if so, where on the body was touching permissible. While observing Smear, it became evident that physical contact was often more than just an incidental part of the experience. The participants would allow themselves to be grabbed by their arms, legs, and/or crotch area before a collapsing into what was described as a "puppy pile." After being tackled, the boys would often linger on the ground, laughing, with their bodies remaining in physical contact. Other times, particularly during lulls in the action, participants would walk around with their arms around each other or, on at least one occasion, were holding hands. The participants were certain that the boys who were physically touching were friends, and that "hanging on," or walking arm in arm, was perfectly acceptable within the context of play. One of the participants commented, "They have their arms around each other because they are friends." Another boy added, "They look like buddies because they are hanging around together."

When asked if that type of touch is permissible outside the context of play, the answers varied by age. The younger the participants, the more likely they were to accept physical closeness as perfectly acceptable. Older players considered the intimate touching that occurred during routine R&T (such as having an arm around another boy) to be permissible only during such play. The boys had a clear sense of what was appropriate touch by a friend within R&T. When shown a videotape of a boy being picked up by a friend who had his hand placed on the boy's derriere, the participants agreed that such touching was okay as long as they were friends and just playing. When asked what they would do if someone who was not a friend touched them like that, they exhibited a clear understanding that such touching outside the play situation was inappropriate. The older boys would be more likely to respond with direct confrontation, whereas the younger boys would be more likely to seek help. The boys made such comments as, "I won't let him do that" or "I would tell the teacher" to the more aggressive "I would get him off" to the very threatening response of "I'll kill him." The intensity of physical contact was markedly different for those who were considered friends versus those who were not friends. Clearly, the boys enjoyed physical contact with their friends; however, that contact was limited primarily to R&T play.

R&T as a Stylized Type of Play

This finding supports Donaldson's (1976) conclusion that R&T is ritualized and symbolic of aggression but not real aggression. The game of Smear followed a predictable rhythm or pattern. The behaviors involved in this game were so routine and predictable that they could be considered almost ritual in nature. Despite the negative appearance of Smear, the participants respected the rules of engagement and the seemingly aggressive yet respectful style of play. Those who did not know the rules or were unfamiliar with the style of play had difficulty playing with those who did. Any interruption in R&T by someone who did not know the rules, or who tried to change them, met resistance from those who routinely engaged in Smear.

Recognizing a play face was something all of the players were able to do. Eye contact and body language clued the players as to whether or not a player was being aggressive. Those exhibiting the play face use smiling, laughing, and eye contact to signal that even though their behavior might appear aggressive, they are still playing (Blurton-Jones, 1976). The Smear players knew the difference between the play face and a truly "aggressive or hostile face." They evaluated eye contact, facial expressions, and body posture to help make this determination. Each one of the informants easily identified what a person looks like when he is angry. Common descriptors included drawn lips, scrunched eyes, furrowed eyebrows, and running too fast. Aggression was further identified by the participants as when a person "has his hands turned inward and arms outstretched like he's going to choke you" and that "his eyes look bad." Those who attempted to play Smear and could not read or missed the nonverbal cues were rejected or ignored.

Players Knew or Observed the Rules

All the regular Smear players knew the rules that governed conduct and behavior. The major rules to Smear, as described by the participants, included: 1) taking turns tackling and being tackled while using only minimal force, 2) retaining possession of the ball when a player falls down accidentally, 3) tending to a player who gets hurt and calling a teacher if needed, 4) waiting until the ball is thrown and caught before tackling a player, 5) chastising a player taking unfair advantage of a fallen player, and 6) recognizing that play face is an integral part of the R&T experience. Since the rules for Smear are not written, players recommitted to them daily. At times, a new rule governing the game would be created, such as a new boundary. Unless embraced by the players, however, the new rule rarely lasted for more than a day.

The rules governing Smear were articulated verbally by older boys and understood by younger ones. The oldest player asserted, "I am the oldest and get to make the rules." Occasionally, an older and more physically developed boy would enter the game and would be granted the allowance of being more physical. The players' knowledge of Smear rules centered on the protection of the players' physical well-being without teacher intervention or direction. Safe zones were created to keep players from being tackled along sidewalks, trees, or other obstructions near the playing field. When a player needed a moment to gather himself, a simple declaration of "time-out" was mutually respected. They also would not use full force, knowing that would be unfair and would increase the possibility of injury.

Knowledge of Rules Separated Players From Intruders

The participants were asked how they knew if a player was an intruder or was going to be aggressive. They were able to detect aggressive players, they said, "Because they start pushing and stuff when they get mean" and because their "eyes would be 'weird.'" One further stated that if "someone is knocking you down and taking the ball, this would not be fair." Other characteristics included frowning, arguing, anger, and retaliating when tackled. When asked what he would do if a person who did not follow the rules fell, one player said he would "just let him lay there and get stepped on." Another boy explained, "We don't get real mad" and "If somebody's not playing fair, sometimes we tell them not to do it." Smear players as a group would try to ignore the intruders, ask them to leave, or as a last resort disband until unwanted player(s) left.

R&T Rarely Results in Injury

An evaluation of the 119 episodes and three hours of R&T reveal only one instance of injury—when one boy stepped into a low spot in the sand and twisted his ankle. This injury resulted from running and not from direct involvement in the bodily contact that is normally associated with R&T. It also occurred at a time when no one was chasing him. Three other players came by to ask if he was okay, while another player,

recognizing that they boy was in pain, scurried off to get a supervisor. The players believed that they would not get hurt playing Smear but also acknowledged that teachers did not like them to play this game because they feared someone would get hurt: "Teachers sometimes don't understand how we play, and they are afraid that we will get hurt."

Discussion

R&T generally, and the game of Smear specifically, appear to be a staging area for caring friendships. To these participants, R&T is also a place for negotiation, problem solving, intimacy, inclusion, and friendly competition. R&T offers opportunities for boys to develop a sense of community that is somewhere between the warmth and closeness of family and the isolation and indifference of the adult masculine world. The observations in this project clearly support both Donaldson's (1976) suggestion that intimate contact is established in R&T and Pellegrini's (1989) assertion that social competence is being developed. Only those boys who were trusted friends and competent in following the rules were welcomed into the game.

Early childhood literature, most notably in the area of developmentally appropriate practice (DAP), seems to have adopted society's taboo against intimate contact among males. Some writers, ignoring the research results, consider R&T to be a form of antisocial behavior (Ladd, 1983) that should be discouraged. In the first edition of the National Association for the Education of Young Children handbook on developmentally appropriate practice, Bredekamp (1986, p. 74) calls for intervention when children "get carried away" with chasing or wrestling. Yet, chasing and wrestling are two salient characteristics of R&T. Ward (1996) suggests that aggressive play should be eliminated, failing to differentiate between real aggression and play that appears aggressive. This attitude may be changing, since the 1997 edition of the developmentally appropriate practice manual suggests that R&T is acceptable, but only for preschool-age children (Bredekamp & Copple, 1997).

The frequently expressed concern that R&T is too rough is not supported by the findings of this study. The only child to be injured in three hours of R&T play turned his ankle when he accidentally stepped in a low spot on the ground. Pellegrini (1989) asserts that aggressive play amounts to less than 5 percent of all play on the playground. Therefore, the likelihood of the often expressed fear that "someone will get hurt" is proven to be low, with the benefits of R&T far outweighing the possibility of injury.

In early childhood, boys are very affectionate and enjoy physical and emotional closeness with their parents (Gilligan, 1982). Gilligan asserts that boys as young as 3 begin a gradual withholding of the outward expression of feelings. Males are taught that "big boys don't cry" and that to "be a man," one must hold in one's feelings. Indeed, being the "strong, silent type" is viewed as an attractive feature. This also may be the point at which males begin to hide their true feelings, and their voices go underground in a similar fashion to what Gilligan (1982) describes for girls. The affectionate and emotionally expressive male finds that being sensitive comes with a price to pay among his peers. As expression of feelings and intimate contact are driven underground, however, they seem to resurface in R&T. Goldstein (1998) suggests that if more men were involved in the giving and receiving of care as an ongoing, central, and valued part of their lives, they would be as likely to espouse such caring as women. R&T appears to be used by boys as camouflage for the expression of intimacy and care for one another.

The very name chosen by the boys for their game, Smear the Queer, is an act of camouflage. Fine (1986) suggests that the word "queer" may be used to indicate "sissy" or "cry baby," rather than a homosexual. In any event, by using the name Smear the Queer, the boys declare that the game is only for the masculine. Yet, the underlying behaviors are in fact acts of intimacy, which in a different context could and probably would be misconstrued as homosexual in nature. The participants, except for the youngest, fully understand that touching each other is only acceptable in the context of play. Unwarranted fear of intimacy among boys (homophobia) may actually retard intimate contact and, consequently, emotional development.

Other findings (gathered from a survey conducted with more than 200 early childhood and elementary teachers) suggest that teachers often interpret R&T play as aggressive, and so they attempt to discourage it (Reed, Brown, & Roth, 2000). These teachers seem to be less interested in potential benefits to children engaging in R&T and more concerned with controlling play. When teachers and administrators deny children the opportunity to participate in R&T, however, they are denying them the opportunity to care for one another. Noddings (1992) emphasizes the need for opportunities to acquire skills in caregiving and to experience care. For boys, care can be expressed in R&T that does not fit within the traditional framework for expressing care. We join Noddings in suggesting that school personnel need to help students increase their self-understanding through reflection on their recreational choices. When boys are denied the opportunity to experience R&T, they are also denied one of the few socially acceptable ways they can express care and intimacy for another male. Miller (1994) refers to such denial of opportunity as poisonous pedagogy, one that, while ostensibly acting in children's best interests, may be doing harm to children.

Implications

An implication of this project is that early childhood and elementary literature should include recommendations to encourage R&T by designing playground space suitable for its rough nature and by allotting time for R&T for those who choose this method of self-expression. Educational programs for administrators and teachers should include information on the difference between R&T and aggressive behavior, and the nature of caring among preadolescent boys. Preservice and inservice educators should be asked to examine society's stereotypes regarding gender and the concept of gender-appropriate behaviors.

Pellegrini (1995) has found play tutoring to be beneficial to the development of children's social, cognitive, and linguistic abilities (Saltz, Dixon, & Johnson, 1977; Smilansky, 1968). Although there are many and varied definitions of play, at least one essential and universal characteristic of play requires that legitimate forms of play (including R&T) must not purposely result in psychological or physical victimization of children (MacDonald, 1992). A child should never be unmercifully teased, pushed around by older or more physically dominating children, verbally abused, or made to perform rituals that are not appropriate for the situation. This is not tolerable. Boulton and Smith (1989) found that confusion between real fighting and play fighting occurred from a misinterpretation of the play signal or because of cheating.

This project and its findings add to the growing body of literature supporting R&T as beneficial for the participants. Such play, as well as other aspects of childhood, needs to be examined in the context of childhood, not adulthood. Educators must learn to evaluate the R&T experience based on its meaning for the participants. As the 21st century unfolds, educators must develop a greater respect for childhood and the rights of children to be childish and to express themselves more openly through play.

References

Blurton-Jones, N. (1976). Rough-and-tumble play among nursery school children. In J. S. Bruner, A. Jolly, & K. Sylva (Eds.), *Play: Its role in development and evolution* (pp. 352-362). New York: Basic Books.

Boulton, M. J., & Smith, P. K. (1989). Issues in the study of children's rough-and-tumble play. In M. N. Bloch & A. D. Pellegrini (Eds.), *The ecological context of children's play* (pp. 57-83). Norwood, NJ: Ablex.

Bredekamp, S. (Ed.). (1986). *Developmentally appropriate practice in early childhood programs from birth through age 8.* Washington, DC: National Association for the Education of Young Children.

Bredekamp, S., & Copple, C. (Eds.). (1997). *Developmentally appropriate practice in early childhood programs.* Washington, DC: National Association for the Education of Young Children.

Bukowski, W., Newcomb, A., & Hartup, W. (Eds.). (1996). *The company they keep: Friendship in childhood and adolescence.* New York: Cambridge University Press.

Burk, D. I. (1996). Understanding friendship and social interaction. *Childhood Education, 72,* 282-285.

Cole, M., John-Steiner, V., Scribner, S., & Souberman. E. (Eds.). (1978). *Mind in society: The development of higher psychological processes.* Cambridge, MA: Harvard University Press.

Conner, K. (1989). Aggression: Is it in the eye of the beholder? *Play and Culture, 2,* 213-217.

Csikszentmihalyi, M. (1975). *Beyond boredom and anxiety: The experience of play in work and games.* San Francisco: Jossey-Bass.

Donaldson, F. (1976). Metacommunication in rough and tumble play. *Reading Improvement, 13,* 235-239.

Fagen, R. (1981). *Animal behavior.* New York: Oxford University Press.

Fine, G. (1986). The dirty play of little boys. *Society, 24*(1), 63-67.

Gilligan, C. (1982). *In a different voice.* Cambridge, MA: Harvard University Press.

Ginsberg, D., Gottman, J., & Parker, J. (1986). The importance of friendship. In J. Gottman & J. Parker (Eds.), *Conversations of friends: Speculations on affective development* (pp. 6-11). London: Cambridge University Press.

Goldstein, L. (1998). Applying the ethic of care. *Journal of Research in Childhood Education, 12,* 247-261.

Harlow, H. (1962). The heterosexual affective system in monkeys. *American Psychologist, 17,* 1-9.

Kochenderfer, B., & Ladd G. (1996). Peer victimization: Manifestations and relations to school adjustment in kindergarten. *Journal of School Psychology, 34*(3), 267-

283.

Ladd, G. (1983). Social networks of popular, average, and rejected children in school settings. *Merrill-Palmer Quarterly, 29*, 283-307.

Lawhon, T. (1997). Encouraging friendships among children. *Childhood Education, 73*, 228-231.

MacDonald, K. (1992). A time and a place for everything: A discrete systems perspective on the role of children's rough and tumble play in educational settings. *Early Education and Development, 3*(4), 334-351.

Merriam-Webster's collegiate dictionary (10th ed.). (1994). Springfield, MA: Merriam-Webster.

Miller, A. (1994). *The drama of the gifted child: The search for the true self.* New York: Basic Books.

Noddings, N. (1992). *The challenge to care in schools: An alternative approach to education.* New York: Teachers College Press.

Oxford American dictionary and language guide. (1999). New York: Oxford University Press.

Pellegrini, A. D. (1989). Elementary school children's rough-and-tumble play. *Early Childhood Research Quarterly, 4*, 245-260.

Pellegrini, A. D. (1994). The rough play of adolescent boys of differing sociometric status. *International Journal of Behavioral Development, 17*(3), 525-540.

Pellegrini, A. D. (1995). A longitudinal study of boys' rough-and-tumble play and dominance during early adolescence. *Journal of Applied Developmental Psychology, 16*, 77-93.

Piaget, J., & Inhelder, B. (1969). *The psychology of the child.* New York: Basic Books.

Reed, T., Brown, M., & Roth, S. (2000). Friendship formation and boys' rough and tumble play: Implications for teacher education programs. *Journal of Early Childhood Teacher Education, 15*(1), 104-116.

Saltz, E., Dixon, D., & Johnson, J. (1977). Training disadvantaged preschoolers on various fantasy activities: Effects on cognitive functioning and impulse control. *Child Development, 48*, 367-380.

Smilansky, S. (1968). *The effects of sociodramatic play on disadvantaged preschool children.* New York: Wiley.

Sutton-Smith, B. (1992). Commentary: At play in the public arena. *Early Education and Development, 3*(4), 390-400.

Ward, C. D. (1996). Adult intervention: Appropriate strategies for enriching the quality of children's play. *Young Children, 51*(3), 20-26.

Section III

The Out-of-Doors: Curriculum Integration

CHAPTER 11

The Out-of-Doors As a Classroom
What Is It?

Cindi Smith-Walters

Cindi Smith-Walters is a professor of biology at Middle Tennessee State University. She is the co-director of the MTSU Environmental Education Center and Assistant Director of the Tennessee Center for the Advancement of Science.

Educators today are held more accountable than ever for student learning, and face increasing pressure to teach more and faster, and to meet local, state, and national standards. Accompanying these mandates is a growing assumption that the classroom "box" is the only place where legitimate learning can occur. As a result, numerous and rich experiences available to students in the outdoor world are being ignored.

Using the outdoors as an integrating context for learning does not have to be primarily focused on learning about the environment, or limited to environmental awareness. Using the outdoors allows educators in both formal (school-type) and informal (e.g., camps, parks, and/or neighborhoods) settings to use natural surroundings and the community as a framework within which students construct their own learning. In these pursuits, students are guided by teachers using proven educational practices. Use of the out-of-doors:

- Breaks down traditional boundaries between disciplines
- Provides hands-on learning experiences (often via problem-solving and project-based activities)
- Allows students with a variety of learning styles and backgrounds to experience success
- Fosters students' skill and ability development
- Develops knowledge, understanding, and appreciation for the entire community and the natural surroundings.

We have all seen (and probably experienced) the excitement accompanying the announcement of a field trip—an experience OUTSIDE of the classroom box. Students have an eager expectation that something fun is going to happen and they are going to be a part of it! This kind of excitement happens daily for youngsters lucky enough to be in classes or groups led by educators who use the great outdoors as their classroom of choice.

Where Exactly Is the Out-of-Doors?
The school ground, a nearby park, a pond, a small stream, a vacant lot, even a neighborhood surrounding a school building can be visited on short jaunts or, if time allows, extended field trips. Such excursions as these enhance learning about traditional school subjects when incorporated into instruction. In today's technology-rich lifestyle, firsthand, meaningful experiences with the natural world are increasingly lacking. Hands-on personal learning experiences in the out-of-doors benefit students. Furthermore, once children are exposed to the out-of-door classroom, they are more apt to continue outdoor active learning beyond their school years (Brown, 1999; Palmer et al., 1998).

Going outside need not be an expensive nor time-consuming project. It may be as simple as planning a windowsill garden, or observing a bird-feeding station near a classroom window. These introductory experiences are small steps that can be expanded upon as teachers build their own repertoires of activities and lessons.

Teachers who want to use natural resources and real-life experiences on an ongoing basis to teach concepts will need to call upon careful and thoughtful planning. All traditional subject and skill areas in the present-day curriculum can be enriched by using the out-of-doors. More important, subject areas become related and integrated when students investigate, interpret, explore, manage, and make decisions about natural resources.

Why Use the Out-Of-Doors?

Youngsters are naturally curious. The brain accumulates and stores information and skills as it performs multiple tasks. All learning, conscious or unconscious, is recorded immediately by changes in the brain's neuron structure. As we analyze complex information and commit it to memory, we also synthesize simple facts into concepts. So, our brain is changed by every act of learning, whether intentional or peripheral, and each person's brain is unique. Initially, we pay primary attention to emotional input. To put it another way, emotionally charged information is absorbed more quickly. The use of play in learning (e.g., the out-of-doors) is a powerful way to link new instruction to students' prior knowledge via emotions (Kotulak, 1996; Sallis et al.,

1999).

For maximum student benefit, outdoor learning experiences are supported with follow-up in the regular classroom. After visiting, exploring, discovering, and investigating in the out-of-doors, students will be excited. Possibly the simplest way for educators to take advantage of this excitement is to have students share their observations and experiences through spoken or written word, drawings, and journal entries. Then, educators can continue to build upon the experience by making use of children's natural inquisitiveness. Children want to learn more about their discoveries, findings, experiences, and investigations. Successful educators facilitate learning by guiding students to enriching books, magazines, films, Web sites, and other resources that expand upon and personalize the outdoor experience.

Benefits:
What Does the Research Say?

A study of 40 schools in the United States in which the environment is used as an "integrating context for learning" (Lieberan & Hoody, 1998) demonstrates the pedagogical advantages of the out-of-doors

The bird habitat offers students opportunities to observe native birds by using binoculars and bird guides. Native plants provide food and shelter while the nearby pond supplies water needed to attract a variety of birds. A single bird house is a good beginning.

approach. Of the 252 teachers participating in the study, the majority reported that when the natural environment was the context for hands-on, project-based learning, student performance improved in the following areas: standardized test scores, grade point average, willingness to stay on-task, adaptability to various learning styles, and problem solving.

The benefits listed above are only those measured within the realm of formal education. Research exploring the antecedents of environmental awareness, sensitivity, commitment, and activism among adults indicates the overwhelming significance of outdoor experiences, especially in childhood (Chawla, 1998). Further research

The Rescue Glade provides a home for the endangered cedar glade. Students locate and transplant cedar glades to the school grounds. Prior to and after the transplanting, this project involved children's inquiry and research skills. Curriculum integration included language arts, science, and geography.

data from nine countries indicate childhood experience in nature proves to be the "most important single factor [in environmental awareness] by far" (Palmer et al., 1998). As part of an increasingly indoor society, many students have limited opportunities for regular, intimate engagement with the natural world. These findings underline the importance of childhood encounters with nature, and the potential benefits of supporting and validating these experiences through schooling (Grant & Littlejohn, 2001).

Longitudinal studies focusing on outcomes of instruction specifically geared to a broad range of learning styles show that with such instruction, students improve learning, are more satisfied with instruction, develop more skill in applying knowledge, and evidence enhanced self-confidence (Chawla, 1998; Palmer et al., 1998). Coupling the outdoor classroom learning experience with an inquiry approach to learning incorporates aspects of varied learning styles and leads to enhanced student achievement.

What About Formal and Informal Activities?

Newcomers to using the outdoors in teaching and learning may want to consult the following two books. Published by the North American Association for Environmental Education (www.naaee.org/npeee/rescource collection-intro.html), they list a variety of resources available to formal and non-formal educators.

The Environmental Education Collection—A Review of Resources for Educators. *1998. ISBN 1-884008-70-7.* This book is designed to help educators find curricula, multimedia resources, and other educational materials that can enhance environmental education in a variety of settings.

Environmental Education in the Schools: Creating a Program That Works! *1994. J. Braus and D. Wood. 500 pages. ISBN 1-884008-08-9.* Ideas to plan an environmental education program or incorporate environmental content into teaching are provided. This comprehensive book includes teaching strategies, fundraising and evaluation tips, resources, and dozens of activities focusing on everything from moral dilemmas to field trips. Originally written for Peace Corps volunteers, the book is valuable to all educators.

Suggested Curricula/Activity Materials

OBIS (Outdoor Biology Instructional Strategies) Berkeley Hall of Science: Delta Educational. These materials are developed for educators without formal education training. They are simple to use and include background information; most are for activities that can be done in the out-of-doors. They also cross-reference to other OBIS activities so that educators can do one or choose several that relate to each other to pursue a unit of study.

The following four international environmental education curriculum programs are highly recommended. These materials have been developed with both formal and informal educators in mind.

Project WILD (Wildlife in Learning Design) K-12 Curriculum and Activity Guide, and Project WILD Aquatic, K-12 Curriculum and Activity Guide. *Administered by the Council for Environmental Education, 2000. CEE, 5555 Morningside Drive, Suite 212, Houston, TX 77005; www.c-e-e.org; www.projectwild.org.* Two collections of activities are arranged by Ecological Knowledge, Social and Political Knowledge, and Sustaining Fish and Wildlife Resources. Activities can stand alone or be used in concert to develop deeper understandings of concepts with students. Cross-referenced and with appendices.

Project Learning Tree—A Supplementary Activity Guide for Grades K Through 8. *American Forest Council, 1111 19th St., NW, Suite 780, Washington, DC 20036; www.plt.org.* This content

provides many excellent activities intended to supplement existing curricula and is arranged according to "story lines." Several activities are grouped around a central core of knowledge and skills relevant to students, providing learners with connectedness and continuity. They are cross-referenced and include appendices.

Project WET (Water Education for Teachers), *201 Culbertson Hall, Montana State University, Bozeman, MT 59717; www.montana.edu/wwwwet.* A collection of innovative, water-related activities that are hands-on, easy to use, and fun. The activities promote critical thinking and problem-solving skills to help students develop into prudent decision-makers regarding water resource use.

Additional Recommendations:

NatureScope, National Wildlife Federation. *8925 Leesburg Pike, Vienna, VA 22184; www.nwf.org.* Wildlife information and activity books for children (60-70 pp. each issue). Includes multi-disciplinary activities, diagrams, photographs, drawings, and reproducibles. Each issue explores a different topic: mammals, birds, wetlands, endangered species, weather, etc.

Homes for Wildlife: A Planning Guide for Habitat Enhancement on School Grounds. *Marilyn C. Wyzga, New Hampshire Fish and Game Department.* Excellent resource for educators who wish to increase the number and kind of wildlife that visit their school grounds and who have an interest in schoolyard mapping, planning, and study.

Schoolyard Habitats: A How-To Guide for K-12 School Communities. *ISBN 0-945051-69-7. National Wildlife Federation, www.nwf.org.* Contains age-appropriate activities and instructional tools to engage students, teachers, and community members in habitat development and will help you create a habitat and enjoy it as an outdoor classroom.

Suggested Books

Cornel, J. (1979). **Sharing Nature With Children** and Cornel, J. (1989). **Sharing the Joy of Nature.** *Nevada City, CA: Dawn Publications. 1-800-545-7475.* Two pocket-size guides helpful to administrators, teachers, and parents. Both are nature-awareness guidebooks with activities for all ages. Each activity is coded by concepts, mood, location, group size, age, and materials. Includes suggestions for teaching. 143 & 167 pp.

Russell, H. R. (1991). **Ten-minute Field Trips: A Teacher's Guide to Using the Schoolgrounds for Environmental Studies.** *Washington, DC: National Science Teachers Association. 1-800-722-NSTA.* An excellent guide with an introduction to each topic, suggested classroom activities, a section on teacher preparation, as well as a cross-referenced listing of field trips for hard-topped school grounds and an annotated list of supplementary materials. 163 pp.

The pond provides children with opportunities to observe, record data, and experience changes throughout the seasons. Students clean out leaves, discuss why fish stay at the bottom of the pond during winter, look under rocks for seasonal changes, and observe the variation of insect and animal life throughout the year. The pond is a complete natural habitat for a nature trail. Children enjoy gathering near the pond for conversation. It serves as an aesthetic backdrop for peer interaction and reflections.

Sisson, E. A. (1982). **Nature With Children of ALL Ages: Activities and Adventures for Exploring, Learning, and Enjoying the World Around Us.** *Upper Saddle River, NJ: Prentice Hall.* Fourteen chapters, arranged by subject (plants, birds, water, etc.), of easy-to-do activities requiring minimal materials. Each chapter has background information, activities with adaptations for different age groups, and a bibliography. 195 pp.

Link, M. (1981). **Outdoor Education: A Manual for Teaching in Nature's Classroom.** *Upper Saddle River, NJ: Prentice Hall.* An excellent book of ideas and suggestions for both experienced and new environmental and outdoor educators.

Roth, C. E., Cervori, C., Wellnitz, T., & Ames, E. (1991). **Beyond the Classroom: Exploration of Schoolyard and Backyard.** *Lincoln, MA: Educational Resources, Massachusetts Audubon Society.* Thirty-three science activities at the elementary level (K-8) requiring a minimal investment of time and equipment. Divided by life science, earth science, and physical science. 64 pp.

Lingelbach, J. (1986). **Hands-on Nature: Information and Activities for Exploring the Environment With Children.** *Woodstock, VT: Vermont Institute of Natural Science.* This idea book of activities and concepts covers adaptations, habitats, cycles, and designs of nature. Each section includes a discussion of concepts, with activities and follow-up. Covers many activities in a general, simplified way, with references for further, in-depth study.

Wilke, Richard (Ed.). (1997). **Environmental Education: A Practical Guide for K-12 Environmental Education.** *Thousand Oaks, CA: Corwin Press.* This book is divided into 13 chapters, which range from integration and curriculum design (planning your curriculum), to finding funding for projects, to curriculum guidelines assessment, ideas for projects, and related children's books.

What Can Teachers Do To Use the Out-of-Doors?

A person cannot learn to write without being actively engaged in the writing process; it is just as impossible to learn to think scientifically without "doing" science. Using the natural world outside the classroom wall is an excellent way to incorporate the "doing" of science and the building of knowledge and skills. *The National Science Education Standards* (1996, p. 113) recommends that educators re-evaluate the what and how of doing science by placing:

LESS EMPHASIS ON

- *knowing scientific facts and information*
- *studying subject matter disciplines (physical, life, earth sciences) for their own sake*
- *implementing inquiry as a set of processes*
- *separating science knowledge and science process*

MORE EMPHASIS ON

- *understanding scientific concepts and developing abilities of inquiry*
- *learning subject matter disciplines in the context of inquiry, technology, science in personal and social perspectives, and the history and nature of science*
- *implementing inquiry as instructional strategies, abilities, and ideas to be learned*
- *integrating all aspects of science content*

How Can Teachers Make It Happen?

Teaching in the out-of-doors should not be another subject added to the curriculum. It is a tool to integrate traditional subject and skill areas as students explore, discover, and investigate their environment. It allows educators to teach the world "together," rather than in small pieces, and it provides students with the knowledge and skills they will use as adults. These are the same skills and knowledge required to make wise decisions about the natural world and our place within it. The real advantage of using the out-of-doors is that firsthand experiences are valued, as opposed to the typical process of teaching with books, chalkboards, and computers.

Many models exist for integrating curriculum via an outdoor classroom. Use of the outdoors as a foundation for learning includes, but is not limited to, lessons in mathematics, language arts, social studies, science, physical education, and the fine arts. Obviously, language arts (reading, writing, communication) is a strong component of all the disciplines. Mathematics and science are natural partners, sharing similar goals of building process and problem-solving skills. Outdoor activities can provide real-life situations, problems, and experimental data to which students can apply the tools of mathematics. Charts and graphing, probability, and statistics are used in studies of populations and ecology, and measurements of mass, volume, distance, and time are needed for most science explorations. Out-of-doors as a classroom makes learning come alive for students.

Anyone with an open mind and a little curiosity can teach, and learn, outdoors. Children and others with inquisitive minds relish sharing learning experiences. Often, parents learn about natural history right along with their children. Teachers and youth group leaders can learn with their children as well! Whether you are a parent, a group leader, a classroom teacher, or work with youngsters in some other situation, don't hesitate to use and participate in outdoor experiences with your children!

References

Brown, B. L. (1999). *Self-efficacy beliefs and career development.* www.ed.gov/databases/ ERIC_Digests/ed429187.html.

Chawla, L. (1998). Significant life experiences revisited: A review of research on sources of environmental sensitivity. *Environmental Education Research, 4*(4), 369-382.

Grant, T., & Littlejohn, G. (Eds.). (2001). *Greening school grounds: Creating habitats for learning.* Gabriola Island, BC, Canada: New Society Publishers.

Kotulak, R. (1996). *Inside the brain: A summary of current research.* Kansas City, KS: Universal Press.

Lieberan, G. A., & Hoody, L. L. (1998). *Closing the achievement gap: Using the environment as an integrating context for learning.* San Diego, CA: State Education and Environment Roundtable.

National Science Teachers Association. (1996). *National science education standards.* Washington, DC: National Academy Press.

Palmer J. A., Suggate, J., Bajd, B., Hart, P., Ho, R. K. P., Ofwono-orecho, J. K. W., Peries, M., Robottom, I., Tsaliki, E., & Van Staden, C. (1998). An overview of significant influences and formative experience on the development of adults' environmental awareness in nine countries. *Environmental Education Research, 4*(4), 445-464.

Sallis, J. F., McKenzie, T. L., Kolody, B., Lewis, M., Marshall, S., & Rosengard, P. (1999). Effects of health related physical education on academic achievement: Project SPARK. *Research Quarterly for Exercise and Sport, 70*(2), 127-34.

CHAPTER 12

Science and Outdoor Play in the Elementary Grades

Christine Chaillé and Xiao-ling Tian

Christine Chaillé is a Professor in the Department of Curriculum and Instruction at Portland State University, Oregon. She co-authored with Lory Britain The Young Child As Scientist: A Constructivist Approach to Early Childhood Science Education. *Xiao-ling Tian taught kindergarten in China for 20 years and is currently a doctoral candidate in Educational Leadership at Portland State University.*

Rivkin (1995) argues that outdoor play is a child's birthright, but that modern society limits and destroys the habitats and access for children's outdoor play. She says that we should "restore children's right to play outside" (p. 10). In terms of science, why should we? What is it that children can learn about science from playing outdoors? In this chapter, we consider the value of children's spontaneous outdoor play for science learning. We use a framework of constructivist science education for considering the value of children's outdoor play as a context in which theory building occurs.

The importance of the outdoors as a place where children learn about science has been recognized for many years. As far back as 1957, experts and educators began to advocate for outdoor education for high school students. Shellenberger (1981) contends that the outdoors is an ideal learning environment for science education. By planning ahead, teachers can provide boundless opportunities for children to explore and observe in the out-of-doors.

Science in the Context of Play

Henniger (1987) talks about play as a hands-on and process-oriented activity. Children's play provides many excellent opportunities for learning fundamental concepts and is an extremely powerful vehicle for learning. By filling and emptying containers, pouring liquid from one to another, children experience the relationships involved in measuring volume. Play also requires creative responses to challenging issues. When children are making sand structures, for example, and the wall collapses, they may discover, through active experimentation and problem solving, that water mixed with the sand will make more durable walls. The atmosphere of play also motivates learning and evokes curiosity and divergent thinking (Chaillé & Silvern, 1996).

Play also is a context for learning to work with others. Hughes (1991) describes play as the vehicle through which children communicate, socialize, learn about the world around them, and understand themselves and others. Morrison (1995) considers communications and interactions among children and between children and adults as critical for language development. When children communicate in the context of their play, and share discoveries with their friends, they are building the social skills of cooperation and communication.

In many regards, then, the outdoors is one of the richest contexts in which play can occur. Perry (2001) believes that the play yard is an arena wherein teachers can plan and implement strategies alongside the events of the peer culture. That is, teachers' planned instruction works in conjunction with the children's spontaneity.

Since play is essential for children's development and learning, outdoor play provides special opportunities for children to learn and grow. Both younger and older children benefit from being outdoors. The different age groups appreciate the broad experiential base provided by being outdoors. In particular, the out-of-doors provides elementary-age children with authentic and relevant opportunities appropriate for their developmental level.

Smith (1995), after six years of observing children's play, found that children play differently in indoor and outdoor environments and play differently with different toys. He also found that in the context of the outdoors, children have much more space and larger apparatus on which to play, and they played more freely and creatively, acquired more useful experience for problem solving, and learned more about social cooperation. Maher (2000) argues that children learn more through outdoor than indoor play; he quotes a student who says, "I learned more in my elementary outdoor classroom than I ever could have in the classroom. The classroom doesn't fit everybody and I am one of those."

Rivkin (2000) and Tyler (2000) contend that the richness and novelty of the outdoors, including traffic, construction, flowing water, moving clouds, animals, etc., and the physical challenge of large-scale or "big" actions, such as shouting, running, climbing, and jumping, stimulate children's development in ways that indoor activities cannot. Outdoors, children are freer to be independent, create new games, solve problems independently, and resolve disputes. They also have opportunities to enact different roles in their play and mentally experience the world from another point of view.

Shellenberger (1981) contends that children need to experience being outside because of the potential for experiences involving all the senses—seeing, hearing, smelling, tasting, and touching—and the increased opportunities for children to manipulate materials while using their senses. Via outdoor play, children can explore, observe, discover, communicate, and compare with materials. Rittner-Heir

Building on children's natural inclination to be out-of-doors, areas are provided to afford a range of learning opportunities.

(2001) uses multiple intelligences theory to point out that bodily-kinesthetic and spatial intelligence are major elements in the learning process for elementary school children; experiences with those intelligences have free rein in the context of outdoor play. Studer (1998) reiterates this point, arguing that children learn best by doing and that outdoor play offers children more opportunities for active multi-sensory learning.

A Framework for Thinking About Science and Outdoor Play

But how do children learn about science in the context of outdoor play? Chaillé and Britain (2003) put forth a framework for constructivist science education that can be used to look at science and outdoor play, a framework using questions that can be seen to underlie children's experimentation and theory-building. We will apply this framework to look at what children learn outdoors. This framework pairs the traditional science content areas of physics, chemistry, and biology/ecology with questions that children ask through their interactions with the world.

Can I Make It Move?

The earliest manifestations of physics, from the constructivist perspective, involve children experimenting with movement of their own bodies and of objects. Opportunities for such experimentation abound in outdoor play. Children in the outdoors are freed from many constraints that exist indoors (Rivkin, 1995). Think about playground experiences involving movement—running, playing ball, and moving in many different ways predominates on the playground. Think also about the facilities available in outdoor play that encourage experimentation with movement—teeter-totters, swings, slides. By playing with slides, swings, teeter-totters, parachutes, balls, and balance beams, children can be introduced to the workings and concepts of pendulums, levers, air pressure, motion, and more (Dreyer &

Bryte, 1990). The swing is a pendulum, and the slide is an inclined plane (Morrison, 1995). A teacher can motivate children to think and explore simply by asking, "Does the steepness of the slide affect how fast toy cars will roll down it?" (Morrison, 1995; Ziemer, 1987). When children try to figure out how the rhythmic rocking of their body might make the swing go higher, they are learning more about cause and effect (Hoorn, Scales, Nourot, & Alward, 1999).

Perry (2001) argues that the outdoors provides less explicit clues and more flexible materials, which can facilitate children's experimentation with movement. Opportunities for playing with objects and materials that move encourage the kind of theory building that is essential for the construction of physical knowledge.

Can I Make It Change?

This is the second question underlying children's early science learning, laying the groundwork for chemistry through experimentation with transformation. Both construction activities, which abound in the outdoors, and opportunities to combine such materials as sand, water, and dirt, provide essential physical knowledge experiences. Rivkin (1995) talks about the significance of "loose parts"—either natural, such as leaves, dirt, and branches, or man-made tools and materials—that children can work and experiment with outdoors. Also, sand, earth, rocks, tree trunks, wood, bricks, and other things in nature provide children with opportunities to test and learn the properties of materials (Hoorn et al., 1999). Children playing outdoors will have the chance to discover differences in texture,

What is this? Is this an example of children's play? Or, is this part of a science lesson? Rather, is this a demonstration of sand art? Answer: All of the above.

color, size, shape, hardness, sound, taste, and smell (Morrison, 1995). Even older children experience these various qualities of different substances. By playing in water, dropping or sinking toys made from different materials (such as plastic boats, containers, wood chips, and toys), children build on earlier experiences and discover multiple physical principles. When children mix sand or dirt with water, they experience changes (colors, shapes, and textures) that affect the materials. When they observe that the sand/dirt they mixed with water is dry again the next day, they learn more reversibility of combinations. They may have opportunities to feel the different temperatures and textures of brick walls, sand, and the sidewalk (Morrison, 1995). These experiences enable elementary children to construct more complex meaning with respect to geography, science, and art.

These early opportunities for children to apply the scientific processes of observing, comparison, and exploration are the essence of science learning (Perry, 2001). Chaillé and Britain (2003) propose two different categories of transformation—constructions and combinations, both of which occur outdoors spontaneously with available and provided materials. As children play outdoors with water, dirt, and sand—pouring, mixing, making different consistencies of mud—they gain an understanding of transformation. And they do so through the kind of unrestricted construction that can occur in a rich outdoor play environment where children have access to materials and the freedom to construct.

How Do I Fit?

This is the third question that children engage in relating to science, and the outdoors provides the context for careful and close observation of the natural world and natural processes. Having the opportunity to experience and closely observe the natural world and the changes that occur in the environment gives children an understanding of the complex relationships in the world, or "ecological perspective-taking" (Chaillé & Britain, 2003). Robin Moore

(1990) argues that these environmental values are fostered by early outdoors experiences. Holt (1991) talks about how science is "a style that leads a person to wonder, to seek, to discover, to know, and then to wonder anew" (p. 181). While playing outdoors, the characteristics of the environment can evoke children's scientific interests and inquiry, enrich children's experiences, and engage them in observing, comparing, and exploring (Morrison, 1995).

Outdoor education, outdoor recreation, environmental education, and experiential education are founded on the values of respect, social responsibility, self-actualization, justice, and freedom for all living beings and the earth (Yerkes & Haras, 1997). Orr (1994) contends that we must educate children to work toward sustaining the cultural and ecological integrity of the places they inhabit; in order to do this, they must know about the ecological patterns, systems of causation, and the long-term effects of human actions on those patterns. From this point of view, it is important for children to play outdoors in order to get acquainted with the ecological environment and to be able to understand these complex concepts (Woodhouse & Knapp, 2000).

Outdoor play also gives children opportunities to learn about the living natural world. Ross (1997), verifying what most teachers know, contends that animals capture the hearts and souls of young children, and children can develop respect and empathy for living things by getting acquainted with the living things in the outdoors. Holt (1991) talks about how such observation and sharing of a reverence for life helps children develop healthy self-concepts. When playing outdoors, children can observe small animals and insects—ants, snails, squirrels, and birds. They can observe the different activities of these animals in different seasons, compare the movement and speed of some small animals, and learn about the particular characteristics of living organisms (Hoorn et al., 1999).

Knapp (1996) suggests that such outdoor play provides natural and built laboratories beyond the school in which to expand and enrich learning. "Outdoor settings present particularly good opportunities for concept development because instruction takes place in 'the real world' " (Resnick, 1989, cited in Knapp, 1992, p. 3). The environment surrounding children when they play outdoors provides opportunities for children to explore, discover, interact, make decisions, create, and think actively. Children use their language to communicate and solve problems; in the process of doing that, they construct knowledge. They are acting in a social context meaningful for them, one in which they are able to create the meanings for themselves.

Swings and Pendulums: An Example of Physics Learning Through Outdoor Play

Let's examine just one example of how playing outdoors fosters science learning. Ruchlis (1974) contends that the playground is a great place for children to observe effects of energy and motion. When children play on the swing, they may notice the swing needs to be pushed in order to start. It will continue to move back and forth, but will finally stop if the pushing ceases. The amount of swinging is greater if one pulls (or pushes) the swing harder before letting go. After these naturally occurring experiences, teachers' explanations or studies of physics in the classroom could mean more to children and help them greatly in understanding the principles of inertia, force and energy, motion, and the reasons that the weight of a child on a swing does not affect the timing of the swing.

Fox (1997) also argues that swings provide an appropriate laboratory in which children experiment with physics principles, such as balance, force, gravity, resistance, and resonance. According to his observations, preschool children first learn how to maintain their balance on the swing. Then they learn how to use their force to keep the swing high or slow it down. When children get skillful on swings, they also learn to use the potential energy, the energy associated with position, to apply force to the swing. Fox's study

(1997) found that children can use kinetic energy (the energy of motion) in seven ways to apply force to start the swing. By experiencing the different swings, children can understand gravity and learn how to get the swing higher to "bump" (the point when the swing is in the highest position where it stops before it swings back down). Children were able to give reasons for why the researcher (Fox) could not get as high as they did. From his observation, children skillfully overcome resistance by putting energy into the swing, and they apply force to make their swing synchronized with another's. Fox concluded that the study of pendulums by older children relates clearly to their earlier experiences on swings, which lays a foundation for constructing a formal understanding of the physics principles associated with pendulums. Furthermore, older children benefit from playing outdoors on swings when they were learning physics principles related to pendulums; the additional swinging experiences help them organize existing information into schemes, thus helping them understand the principles better.

This is but one example of how science learning happens through children's outdoor play. By increasing teachers' awareness and understanding of how children engage in such learning, such opportunities can be facilitated and extended into the classroom, and classroom experiences can extend into the outdoors.

References

Chaillé, C., & Britain, L. (2003). *The young child as scientist: A constructivist approach to early childhood science education.* New York: Allyn & Bacon.

Chaillé, C., & Silvern, S. (1996). Understanding through play. *Childhood Education, 72,* 274-277.

Dreyer, K. J., & Bryte, J. (1990). Slides, swings, and science. *Science and Children, 27*(7), 36-37.

Fox, J. E. (1997). Swinging: What young children begin to learn about physics during outdoor play. *Journal of Elementary Science Education, 9*(1), 1-14.

Henniger, M. L. (1987). Learning mathematics

and science through play. *Childhood Education, 63*, 167-171.

Holt, B. (1991). *Science with young children.* Washington, DC: National Association for the Education of Young Children.

Hoorn, J. V., Scales, B., Nourot, P. M., & Alward, K. R. (1999). *Play at the center of the curriculum.* Columbus, OH: Prentice Hall,

Hughes, F. P. (1991). *Children, play and development.* Boston: Allyn & Bacon.

Knapp, C. E. (1992). Thinking in outdoor inquiry. *ERIC Digest* (Report No. EDO-RC-92-3). Charleston, WV: ERIC Clearinghouse on Rural Education and Small Schools. (ERIC Document Reproduction Service No. ED 348198)

Knapp, C. E. (1996). *Just beyond the classroom: Community adventures for interdisciplinary learning.* (Report No. EDO-RC-92-3). Charleston, WV: ERIC Clearinghouse on Rural Education and Small Schools. (ERIC Document Reproduction Service No. ED 388 485)

Maher, K. J. (2000). Outdoor classroom adventures. *Science and Children, 37*(5), 20-23.

Moore, R. (1990). *Childhood's domain.* Berkeley, CA: MIG Communications.

Morrison, K. (1995). Science by discovery. *Texas Child Care, 19*(2), 22-26.

Orr, D. W. (1994). *Earth in mind: On education environment and the human prospect.* Washington, DC: Island Press.

Perry, J. P. (2001). *Outdoor play, teaching strategies with young children.* New York: Teachers College Press.

Rittner-Heir, R. M. (2001). Playgrounds: They're not just for fun anymore. *School Planning & Management, 40*(3), 61-64.

Rivkin, M. S. (1995). *The great outdoors: Restoring children's right to play outside.* Washington, DC: National Association for the Education of Young Children.

Rivkin, M. S. (2000). *Outdoor experiences for young children.* (Report No. EDO-RC-00-7). West Virginia, U. S. (ERIC Document Reproduction Service No. ED 448013)

Ross, M. E. (1997). Scientists at play. *Science and Children, 34*(8), 35-38.

Ruchlis, H. (1974). Playground physics. *Science and Children, 11*(8), 21-23.

Shellenberger, B. R. (1981). Take your class outdoors! *Science and Children, 19*(2), 28-29

Smith, P. K. (1995). Play, ethnology and education: A personal account. In A. D. Pellegrini (Eds.), *The future of play theory: A multidisciplinary inquiry into the contributions of Brian Sutton-Smith* (pp. 3-21). Albany, NY: State University of New York.

Studer, M. L. (1998). Blending classroom curriculum and outdoor play space. *Texas Child Care, 2*(1), 12-19.

Tyler, V. (2000). Why recess? *Dimensions of Early Childhood, 28*(4), 21-23.

Woodhouse, J., & Knapp, C. E. (2000). *Place-based curriculum and instruction: Outdoor and environmental education approaches* (Report No. EDO-RC-00-6). West Virginia. (ERIC Document Reproduction Service No. ED 448012)

Yerkes, R., & Haras, K. (1997). Outdoor education and environmental responsibility *ERIC Digest.* (Report No. EDO-RC-97-6). West Virginia. (ERIC Document Reproduction Service No. ED 414112)

Ziemer, M. (1987). Science and the early childhood curriculum: One thing leads to another. *Young Children, 42*(6), 44-51.

CHAPTER 13

Social Studies in the Outdoors? You've GOT To Be Kidding!

William M. Stone and Sandra J. Stone

*William M. Stone is a clinical instructor at Northern Arizona University (NAU)
in Flagstaff, Arizona. He taught in elementary school settings for 20 years and
served as a curriculum specialist for 10 years before moving to the university
setting. He now teaches social studies and science methods courses at the
College of Education. Sandra J. Stone, a professor also at NAU, has authored
several books and articles, including the books* Playing: A Kid's Curriculum
(GoodYear Books, 1993) and Creating the Multiage Classroom *(GoodYear Books,
1996). She directs the National Multiage Institute and the
NAU Professional Development School Program.*

W hen one thinks about social studies, what usually comes to mind is reading in a textbook about social studies, possibly about the exports and imports of Argentina, and then answering the questions at the back of the chapter. Of course, there is a test on Friday. The idea of teaching social studies in the outdoors very likely would elicit a response of unbelief, or skepticism at the very least. "You've GOT to be kidding!" is one possible response.

Upon further review, however, a few thoughts do come to mind regarding how social studies could be taught outside the classroom. Field trips are the most obvious ways to teach social studies. A teacher might take the class to the local city hall or state capitol to observe the functions of government, or to a museum to see how past cultures have shaped our lives today. At a retail store or factory, children can learn the principles of economics, such as the production and consumption of goods or supply and demand.

Another idea may occur regarding the teaching of social skills. As children play together outdoors at recess, they are obeying rules, taking turns, practicing conflict resolution, and engaging in open communication, etc. And, of course, kudos go to the occasional teacher who buries chicken bones in the playground sand pit, and takes the students out for an exciting anthropological "dig."

Beyond these obvious methods, however, is it possible to delve further into the social studies as we move our children outside the walls of the classroom? The answer is a resounding "Yes!"

To find successful ways of teaching social studies in an outdoor setting, it is important to look closely at the definition of social studies. According to the National Council for the Social Studies (NCSS) (1994), all elements of social studies point to the ultimate goal of promoting civic competence. What exactly does that mean? NCSS defines it in the context of the main goal for teachers, which is to help children develop the ability to make informed and reasoned decisions for the public good as citizens of a culturally diverse, democratic society in an interdependent world.

The definition of social studies does not so much address the call for a curriculum that emphasizes factual knowledge as it begs for teachers to help children become good citizens, capable of thinking critically, communicating well, solving problems, and making reflective decisions. We study people and cultures, past, present, and future, not only to learn tolerance, acceptance, and understanding of all people, but also to develop our own character as individuals and as citizens of society.

Second, it is fairly safe to assume that in order to effectively teach the skills that can lead to civic competence, students must have the opportunity to practice such skills. The implication for teachers is that we must give our children the opportunity to be involved in open dialogue and communication, using higher order thinking skills. We must allow our children to make real decisions based on real-world problems.

So what does this all have to do with being outdoors? According to the constructivist approach, the construction of knowledge is built upon prior experience. Students learn not only by experience, but also from experience; a search for meaning must accompany the experience. The classroom is hardly a place to provide such life experiences, as it is artificial and contrived at best. Outdoor learning is a more naturalistic approach, allowing for greater freedom of imagination and thought. John Dewey (1916) understood the importance of experiential learning. He stated that learning should be concrete and that it should be as "unscholastic" as possible. Artificial ways of learning, such as textbooks, workbooks, and lesson plans, were a "waste of time." He advised teachers who want experiential learning for their students to call to mind the kinds of situations that occur outside the school. It seems that we can take this one step further, not only calling to mind those situations, but to actually experience them and placing the learning process in contexts that are as meaningful as possible.

Third, very little has been written about using the outdoors as a setting for teaching social studies or for children playing with social studies themes. While a great deal of information about outdoor education is available, much of what has been written focuses on the environment and emphasizes the sciences. Therefore, it is important to explore the possibilities that the out-of-doors offer for teaching social studies and for social studies play.

Play and Outdoor Education

Play, including outdoor play, is a tremendous and powerful tool in the process of children's learning (Frost, 1997; Stone, 1995; Strickland, 2002). Much has been written on the benefits of play as a learning tool. Isenberg and Quisenberry (2002) believe that "play—a dynamic, active, and constructive behavior—is an essential and integral part of all children's healthy growth, development, and learning across all ages, domains, and culture" (p. 33). Play settings can provide critical experiential foundations as children construct their own knowledge of how the world works. Isenberg and Quisenberry support this claim by stating that "no program of adult instruction can substitute for children's own observations, activities, and direct knowledge" (p. 35).

Thus, play is delineated from other learning experiences wherein the teacher sets the goals. To be considered a play experience, the child must freely choose the play and the process takes precedence over the product. The child is in charge; he is autonomous. Through play, the child is able to move beyond literal reality, and then has the freedom to experiment, create, and invent new possibilities. Outdoor play creates a context that allows children to solve problems (Rivkin, 2001) and become reflective decision makers.

On the other hand, while outdoor education may include play, most often it is hands-on, active learning promoted by the teacher. Outdoor education first was advocated during the time of the American Civil War. Colonel Francis Parker, a former schoolteacher, questioned what children were learning when they were sitting quietly on hard benches with their eyes and attention focused on arbitrarily chosen textbooks. He suggested that teachers take their students outside, where they could learn about "real life." John Dewey, as mentioned earlier, certainly concurred.

Although it received little attention at the time, Lynn Cook (1999) describes the importance of the 1944 Education Act, which encouraged education authorities to maximize the use of the outdoors for educational purposes. Proponents of the act believed outdoor education would improve the health of children, give them experience of the country, enhance the curriculum, and develop character. Gary McCulloch also mentions the 1944 Education Act (Cook, 1999), explaining that outdoor education can create a context wherein adults can mold the behaviors of adolescents so their characters and energies can be channeled into new and positive directions. Thus, outdoor education provided a context for children to learn tolerance, acceptance, and understanding of people, as well as helping them develop their own character and develop as citizens of society.

Numerous organizations currently focus their attention on outdoor education, including the Coalition for Education in the Outdoors, Outward Bound, and the Foxfire Approach. Public schools all across the United States are recognizing the importance of outdoor education. Some use the expertise of professional organizations, such as the Boojum Institute for Experiential Education, to assist in the development of outdoor education programs. Many schools also are developing their own outdoor education programs, such as the program created by the Crossroads School in Santa Monica, California, and Camp Colton in Flagstaff, Arizona. All of these programs are designed to engage students in the learning process by helping them to pose and solve problems, explore issues, take risks, and learn to cooperate with one another. Through these programs, students benefit by becoming more self-reliant and confident, which leads to greater communication skills, responsibility, and self-esteem. What better social studies skills are there?

Redirecting schools from the inside to the outside simply increases the learning environment and provides greater opportunities for children to learn both in and through the outdoors. Outdoor learning provides unlimited possibilities for children to become good citizens.

Practical Strategies for Implementing Social Studies Out-of-Doors

The authors, in recognizing the difference between play and planned learning experiences, present strategies and ideas for both. Outdoor play experiences allow the children to use materials to invent and create within a social studies context. The outcomes of the play are determined by the children. However, the children are still playing through social studies contexts. Outdoor learning experiences, on the other hand, may be planned by the teacher and/or the children with a more specific social studies goal in mind.

Outdoor Play Experiences

Play Stations. The play centers typical for primary children become play "stations" for intermediate children. A number of play stations can be created outside (Kruglik, 1993). Some of these stations may be permanent and others may be portable (transported to the outside from the inside). The play in these stations is open-ended and ongoing, and allows concepts to be applied (Brown, 1998). Children also can integrate stations. Keep in mind that while these play stations could occur within the intermediate classroom, by placing them outside, the play becomes larger, more adventuresome, and non-traditional.

• *Anthropology Station.* Possibilities for play in this station include creating a culture; making contact with another culture; producing artifacts; developing a language, shelter, clothing, traditions, and philosophy; and establishing rules and government.

• *Economics Station.* Economists address the problem of scarce materials and resources. Choices are made about the consumption of goods and the delivery of services. Possibilities for play include creating a store, creating a barter system, making the goods or deciding on the services sold, deciding the demand (need, wish, or ability to purchase goods and services), deciding the division of labor (assigning tasks to workers), analyzing profit, and creating a corporation in which people invest money and share in profits and losses. Inside the classroom, you might see a bank or a grocery store; outside the classroom, you could see a plant nursery, lumberyard, car repair shop, or power plant. Be sure to provide ample building materials and tools.

• *Geography Station.* Possibilities for this station include developing maps, and describing places or phenomena. Children can create regions, environments, and cultures in dirt or sand, and then map and describe their creations. Details of the created areas may include topography, climate, soil, vegetation, transportation, and relationships with other regions. Tools for digging, planting, and building would be available for the children to use.

• *History Station.* This station can involve reenactments or depictions of historical or current events and the building of museums and displays. Children can create how people during different time periods built their homes, sold their wares, grew their food, lived, and died. Cardboard boxes, wood, and outdoor tools are on hand for the creations.

• *Sociology Station.* Sociology studies human beings and their groups, norms, and behaviors. Children's understandings of these groups is embedded in play that includes families, tribes, a society, or an entire nation. Groups can include suburban dwellers, migrant workers, or politicians. Children have a chance to try out different social norms and values.

• *Political Science Station.* In this station, children set up political systems, governments, laws, and international relations. Regions and countries can be established on the playground. Some of the play can be extended into the classroom (for instance, by holding elections), but the outdoors is the base of the play.

Themes for the play stations can be changed throughout the year, and can range from prehistoric to current events, Roman history to the American Revolution. As the context changes, so will the experiences within the outdoor stations. Open-ended materials, such as boxes, can have multiple uses. What may have been a building in a city can become a cave during prehistoric times.

Adventure Playgrounds. Adventure playgrounds allow older children to play out social stories and establish social relationships with other children. Adventure playgrounds can be developed by adults or by the students themselves with the help of adults. These playgrounds use the natural environment and discarded materials. Children can tear down, build, and rebuild their own play environments. Natural materials may include mud, ponds, gardens, sand areas, etc. Discarded materials could include lumber, boxes, ropes, tires, ramps, and building tools such as hammers and nails. Here are some guidelines:

• Use flexible materials
• Provide linkages to other playground equipment
• Promote a wide variety of experiences
• Provide close adult supervision to decrease safety concerns. (Johnson, Christie, & Yawkey, 1999)

Adventure Playgrounds, which are as safe as traditional playgrounds, allow children to create, invent, and use social and higher order thinking skills for authentic reasons. Possibilities for social play in these environments can be suggested by the teacher or the children; however, the choice is the children's to make. For example, children may choose to use the materials to reenact the siege at the Alamo, create a community or Old West Town from the 1800s, or play out such historical fiction books as *Lackawanna* (Chester Aaron), *Number the Stars* (Lois Lowry), and *Sounder* (William H. Armstrong).

Outdoor Games. Playing outdoor games promotes social development, fairness, negotiation, resolving conflict, and turn-taking. Social games include the traditional games of baseball, basketball, jacks, and jump rope. Another way to use the outdoors with games is to explore historical or cultural games. Have the children find out when games originated, where they were played in the world, and how the rules have changed. Create game groups to try out historical and cultural games and teach them to others.

Outdoor play has many benefits for elementary and middle school children. It builds confidence, encourages children to solve problems that have meaning for them (Strickland, 2001), provides opportunities for creative and reflective thinking, and helps children to work and play cooperatively.

Outdoor Learning Experiences

Teachers and/or students may plan outdoor learning experiences for a specific goal, such as learning how government works, engaging in responsible civic behaviors, or learning how a business grows and develops. Listed below are ways to deliberately use the out-of-doors through planned learning experiences.

Service Projects. Service projects are an excellent way to provide real opportunities for civic responsibility. Teachers and students can investigate possibilities for an outdoor service project in their own community. The project may only require a small amount of time and research, or it could be something that the children would work on for an entire year, changing and implementing new ideas as the project continues.

For example, at a school in Tucson, Arizona, that was situated by an empty, littered lot, a 5th-grade class decided to make the lot more appealing and useful for the surrounding community. To transform this eyesore, the students got the issue on the agenda of the next city council meeting. Before the meeting, they took photographs of the lot to use when presenting their case to the council members. They also developed a plan to pick up the litter in the lot; plant trees, shrubs, and grass; and turn the lot into a small park. The city, which owned the lot, agreed with the students and gave the go-ahead for the plan developed by the students. The actual work took several months. The students secured donations for plants and seeds from local businesses. Finally, when the project was complete, the students had a ribbon-cutting event that was attended by the community and covered by newspaper and television reporters.

Another class, in Washington state, decided to clean up a local creek. The creek once had been a place where salmon would come to lay their eggs; due to pollution and litter, however, the fish had stopped coming. The students worked with the community to clean up the creek, made "No Littering" signs, and then raised thousands of salmon eggs in a class

Workstations in close proximity provide teachers and students with places to work cooperatively, record data, and discuss observations.

aquarium to place in the cleaned-up creek (Ellis, 1998).

A class in California decided to join a "get-out-to-vote" campaign. Accompanied by parents, the students distributed flyers door-to-door in their neighborhoods. The hand-made flyers encouraged adults to register and vote (Muir, 1996). Another social studies project, undertaken by a 4th-grade class, focused on the elderly residents in their neighborhood. The students "adopted" several residents and helped them throughout the year with yard work and errands.

Students also could do service projects focusing on increasing wheelchair accessibility in the community, cleaning up graffiti, preserving a historical place, increasing awareness on a controversial topic, or assisting with a local archeological dig. Many community service organizations, such as 4-H, Camp Fire, and League of Women Voters, as well as a variety of books (Lewis, 1991, 1995), would be helpful in organizing such service projects.

Field Trips. Of course, field trips are an excellent outdoor experience for intermediate students. Investigate outdoor places in your own community or nearby communities that would be accessible for a field trip. Some communities have historical settings that are specifically set up for elementary school field trips. Think of the usual places that reflect social studies, but also consider more unusual places. Out-of-the-way places, such as an old graveyard, can be outstanding field trip opportunities. Here is a list of possibilities for field trips:

Protected animal habitat areas
Homes or commercial buildings under
    construction
Grocery store
Chicken farm
Egg production farm
Places of transportation: airport, bus
    terminal, ferry
Museums: history, culture, machines, cars
Government offices: courts, legislative
    offices, police stations
Newspaper publishing offices

Mining community: mines, mine offices
Old graveyard
Old building in town still in use
Vegetable farm

Outdoor Projects. The project approach (Katz & Chard, 1991) describes projects as a way to engage students' minds, encourage their interactions with people, objects, and the environment in ways that are meaningful, and to use their skills for real reasons. Social studies projects in the outdoors give new meaning to a hands-on approach. For example, students could turn a field trip to a train station into creating a model train station and community outside the classroom, complete with the history of the station and how it served people many years ago. A visit to a historical habitat such as the Anasazi site at Walnut Canyon in Flagstaff, Arizona, could inspire students to build a replica environment.

Students could create outdoor job areas in the playground, ranging from a plant nursery to a wood working shop. The economics involved in deciding on an outdoor business, hiring people, managing money, making a profit, and keeping the books would be exciting and beneficial to the students' understanding of how economics functions in society.

Other great outdoor projects include drawing life-size dinosaurs on the basketball court, labeling the school with map symbols and directions, and building a statue to represent someone important in the community. Students also can use the outdoors to make models of communities, such as the students' own town, as they looked 50 years, 100 years ago, etc. Students could re-create the story of *Roxaboxen* (Alice McLerran), in which a young girl used rocks to represent where she lived. Students can build various shelters (such as igloos, highrises, and longhouses) or build models of various historical methods of transportation (such as oxcarts, prairie schooners, ships, canoes, or early automobiles). Students can experiment with building materials, such as making adobe blocks used by early settlers in the West.

Inquiry Projects. Inquiry projects begin with students asking questions and then generating hypotheses. Through their investigative projects, they discard, add to, or revise their hypotheses. Inquiry projects could begin with questions such as, "Why did the Romans use aqueducts?" and "How do aqueducts work?" As an inquiry project, students can hypothesize their own ways to get water from one place to another on the playground, actually build aqueducts, and then compare their experiences with their findings from research of the Roman aqueducts. Students could problem-solve such transportation issues as how to build a bridge over a harbor so that a ship could pass through. After they build their own inventions outside, they could research how others have solved this problem. For example, Leonardo DaVinci designed a moving bridge that was later used by architects to build a bridge that is currently in use in Curaçao in the Netherlands Antilles.

Another line of inquiry could be simply investigating whether or not playground games are democratic. Students can make their guesses and then collect data through observation, a questionnaire and a survey instrument that they would have designed. Outdoor inquiry projects give children the opportunity to ask questions that require an outside context and greater room to try out their hypotheses.

Outdoor Experiences. Outdoor social studies experiences can offer another way to involve students in exciting, challenging, and meaningful learning. For example, students can examine cultures by forming teams whereby each team creates a culture and then buries artifacts on the school grounds. Each team then excavates and analyzes the other team's artifacts and uses them to reconstruct its culture. The process of this outdoor experience deepens the students' understanding of past cultures and the work of anthropologists while giving a context; students must actively think rather than memorize facts.

Role-playing historical events, such as the Boston Tea Party, is another outdoor possibility that allows students to experience not only the event but also the emotion behind the event. Outdoor experiences may include simulations—a strategy that tries to replicate the event or process as closely to the essential characteristics of the real thing as possible (Parker & Jarolimek, 1997). Simulations are elaborate role-play and they allow students to make decisions similar to those that people actually have to make in real life. For example, one outside simulation could be participating in assembly line practices. The children would choose a product, such as a simple birdhouse. Once outside, they would set up the "factory." The students would decide on the materials and workers needed and then diagram the process. One person may be the pattern tracer, another two people could be the cutters, and one more person would take the role of paster, etc. Through the experience of actually building birdhouses on an assembly line, the students can answer questions, such as, "Do assembly workers become bored?" or "Do you think the workers take pride in their work?" How much better for students to experience this process rather than simply read about the concept of assembly line production in a unit on the growth of industry (Parker & Jarolimek, 1997).

Teaching social studies outdoors may at first glance elicit the response, "You've GOT to be kidding!" When you really think about it, however, would you rather have children involved only in textbooks and worksheets or in really living social studies? Outdoor social studies experiences offer, as Dewey (1916) suggests, concrete forms of learning, which are as "unscholastic" as possible. Moving social studies outdoors gives learning a more naturalistic approach, which can significantly enhance the goals of social studies. These goals include developing decision-makers who can think critically, solve problems, and understand others with the ultimate goal of promoting civic competence (National Council for the Social Studies, 1994). Think outside the box; think "outdoors" when planning your next social studies experience. We're not kidding!

Reference

Brown, R. G. (1998). Outdoor learning centers: Realistic social studies experiences for K-6 students. *Social Studies, 89*(5), 199-205.

Cook, L. (1999). The 1994 Education Act and outdoor education: From policy to practice. *History of Education, 28*(2), 157-172.

Dewey, J. (1916). *Democracy in education.* New York: Macmillan.

Ellis, A. K. (1998). *Teaching and learning elementary social studies.* Boston: Allyn and Bacon.

Frost, J. L. (1997). Child development and playgrounds. *Parks & Recreation, 32*(4), 54-61.

Isenberg, J. P., & Quisenberry, N. (2002). Play: Essential for all children. *Childhood Education, 79*, 33-39.

Johnson, J. E., Christie, J. F., & Yawkey, T. D. (1999). *Play and early childhood development.* New York: Addison Wesley Longman.

Katz, L. G., & Chard, S. C. (1991). *Engaging children's minds: The project approach.* Norwood, NJ: Ablex.

Kruglik, M. (1993). Students are turning an empty lot into an outdoor learning center. *Curriculum Review, 33*(4), 8.

Lewis, B. A. (1991). *The kid's guide to social action: How to solve the social problems you choose, and turn creative thinking into positive action.* Minneapolis, MN: Free Spirit Publishing.

Lewis, B. A. (1995). *The kid's guide to service projects: Over 500 service ideas for young people who want to make a difference.* Minneapolis, MN: Free Spirit Publishing.

Muir, S. P. (1996). Simulations for elementary and primary school social studies: An annotated bibliography. *Simulation and Gaming: An International Journal of Theory, Practice, and Research, 7*, 41-73.

National Council for the Social Studies Task Force on Curriculum Standards for the Social Studies. (1994). *Expectations of excellence: Curriculum standards for social studies: Bulletin 89.* Washington, DC: National Council for the Social Studies.

Parker, W. C., & Jarolimek, J. (1997). *Social studies in elementary education.* Columbus, OH: Merrill/Prentice-Hall.

Rivkin, M. S. (2001). Problem solving through outdoor play. *Early Childhood Today, 15*(7), 36-44.

Stone, S. J. (1995). Wanted: Advocates for play in the primary grades. *Young Children, 50*(6), 45-54.

Strickland, E. (2001). What children learn through outdoor play. *Early Childhood Today, 15*(7), 44.

Strickland, E. (2002). Eric Strickland, Ph.D., on exploring the benefits of outdoor play. *Early Childhood Today, 16*(8), 44.

CHAPTER 14

Arts and the Out-of-Doors

Joanne Curran

Joanne Curran is currently Assistant Dean of Education at SUNY College at Oneonta, New York. She is also an Associate Professor of Educational Psychology and a colleague of the Creative Education Foundation.

G etting out—out of the usual, out of the ordinary, out of the box, out of our minds (mindsets, that is)—is one of the goals of the creative arts. Perceiving, thinking, and experiencing in new and different ways assists in the development of the critical thinking skills necessary for school success. Going outside, both literally and figuratively, promotes creative thinking and helps teachers and children see the world as their classroom.

Tony Poze and William Gordon, the creators of Synectics Inc., a creative thinking model, spoke of making the strange familiar and making the familiar strange as an accordion-like creative process of learning and innovation (Gordon & Poze, 1972). They proposed three ways to promote creative thinking. First, learning to make comparisons helps a person to either understand something or invent something new. For example, students are asked, "What mechanical thing acts like an angry snake?" Second, students are encouraged to "be" something they are not. This is really an exercise in perspective taking. Students "become" a fly or a tree or anything other than themselves. For example, students are asked, "What in nature should we copy to learn how to be patient?" (Gordon & Poze, 1972, p. 42) and "Imagine you are a mouse caught in a forest fire. What action would you take to escape?" (p. 43). Students are encouraged to use metaphors from the mechanical and natural worlds to solve problems. Third, students are asked to create "stretched comparisons" or "compressed conflicts" (p. 84). These are comparisons of apparently dissimilar objects (e.g., "sad smile") that focus on a deeper and richer real meaning. When we make the strange familiar, and when we make the familiar strange, we add to our thinking repertoire. Piaget (1955) described this process as the assimilation and accommodation of adaptation. When we take our students outside the traditional classroom, we help them experience and construct learning in new ways.

Taking children outside the walls of a classroom allows us to teach them to see the world with the eye of an artist (Loughran, 2001). Sometimes we limit our thinking about art to a product. Art first requires a new way of seeing and thinking about the environment. Going outside provides opportunities for children to see how the natural environment inspires the man-made environment. Patterns in nature are duplicated in architectural design, clothing design, and even simple doodling. The balance and harmony seen in nature is duplicated in music, art, drama, and dance as components, and their intricate relationships are recognized.

One of the first steps in art education is learning to see. Frederick Franck (1979) has inspired many novice artists by teaching the "zen of seeing/drawing," whereby students are instructed to avoid looking at their paper while drawing—keeping your eyes on the subject helps you learn to really see it. The optimum place for learning to see and draw is, yes, outside. Franck developed an art form that combines both drawing and meditation by asking novice artists to look deeply at the subject of the drawing. He told students to look at the subject, not the paper, to really see what it was they had chosen to draw. The first step is literally to draw without looking away from the subject. For the second draft, one looks at the paper some, but continues to focus attention on the subject.

This shift in thinking from product to process, from their drawing to the recognition of elements of the subject to be drawn, assists the novice artist in learning to see and learning to delay judgment or evaluation. It is through this delay in evaluation that real learning can take place. But don't mistake delay for neglect. Evaluation is important, but must be conducted at the appropriate time, with the intention of improvement rather than judgment. Very young children can become frustrated with drawing when they recognize that their work does not clearly represent the subject. As children get older, they begin to make social comparisons. Many decide that they "can't draw" when they evaluate their own work too quickly and in relative terms to their peers. Taking them outside and using a novel set of materials helps them delay the evaluative portion of the process. Focusing on the subject rather than their depiction of the subject has surprised many novice artists, young and old. Nothing is more rewarding than helping someone recognize his or her own ability.

The Museum of Outdoor Arts is a physical manifestation of the idea of changing our thinking about

the arts by going outside. Its mission statement illustrates the power of making the familiar strange, with "artists working in styles and media that redefine the form and content of art through risk-taking and innovation, exhibits that draw the viewer by reinterpreting our view of reality, expanding our appreciation of the commonplace, taking us to exotic places or asking that we respond actively rather than passively to the new and unfamiliar" (www.moaonline.org). An innovative classroom teacher can create his or her own Museum of Outdoor Arts by looking carefully at the following three practices associated with the arts outdoors and integrating these practices with other subject areas in the classroom.

Built Environments

Proponents of outdoor education advocate envisioning the out-of-doors as a "potential space" of creativity and imagination (Moore & Wong, 1997, p. 197). In a 10-year, action research project called The Environmental Yard, Moore and Wong described the transformation of an asphalt, urban schoolyard into a community open space. This space became a rich, educational resource for an elementary school and its greater community as teachers

When in the out-of-doors, children find natural materials with which to play, construct, and create.

moved from inside the classrooms to outside and learned to see through the eyes of children. Not only did both teachers and children learn to really see what was in their world, they also established together a "sense of place" (p. 65). The researchers described this sense of place as a feeling of belonging to a particular physical space that is different from any other space, a space to which they belong in a special way. What happens in a special place is dramatic, motivating, and unforgettable. In addition to the traditional emphasis of outdoor education on the natural sciences, the researchers reported activities related to dance, visual arts, photography, and theater.

Playgrounds are only one kind of built environment, however. Teachers can lead the way to construct classroom gardens, involving children in the design and planting as well as tending to a variety of plants. Other examples of built environments include the traditional "forts" and tree houses, as well as rinks for skating and platforms for performances. One final example, based in part on a special location, allows for children to visit and participate in the renovations of a historical farmhouse that just happens to be next to their school.

Found Objects

Found art refers to any artistic work that is made up of either natural or salvaged objects (Ruggiero, 1981). Nearly all primitive art is classified as found art, and the materials incorporated are referred to as found objects (Stribling, 1970). Modern art of the 1950s and 1960s saw a whole generation of artists using found objects or "trash" in a wide variety of forms. Jasper Johns incorporated flags and paintbrushes. Joseph Cornell created boxes filled with carefully chosen objects (Slesin, 1981). Children have been called "natural junk artists" (Rasmusen & Grant, 1967, p. 97). Junk sculptures are especially helpful when working with older children, including those who have decided that they "can't draw" or have little talent. Field trips to places where discarded objects might be found assist children in becoming involved in the project. Challenge students to seek out objects in the neighborhood around school. These found objects can become part of a visual arts collage or sculpture. Found objects can find their way into poetry or be used as props for improvisational theater.

Found objects are gaining an important place in cultural anthropology as well. Anthropologists are investigating garbage dumps to draw some conclusions about what is valued in a culture. Children, too, can learn to make some assumptions about what products we tend to throw away, while using those same objects to make a statement about what is wasted and what is valued in a community.

The amphitheater provides a gathering place for large group instruction, culminating activities, and outdoor programs.

Documentaries

Children can leave the classroom in order to collect information about themselves and their community. Photography allows children to select topics that might surprise teachers. Mueller (1993) gave children disposable cameras and told them to take pictures of anything they wanted. She was surprised to discover that the children, without guile, documented their homes, families, and even gang signs displayed by older siblings. The children then developed photo essays and written essays about themselves. In this case, the teachers learned to "see" their students in a new way. Teachers were able to see beyond the child-in-the-classroom to the child-in-the-family/neighborhood. The children's home experiences became part of the classroom canon, and their experiences were validated because of this inclusion.

Children can complete oral histories by talking with people in their communities and writing down or videotaping the stories they hear. Getting out into the real world also helps children to take responsibility for their learning and helps them see the connections between what happens in the classroom and what happens in the world beyond.

As the world outside the classroom becomes a familiar place for learning and exploring, the classroom itself may become strange. Creating a different space for learning is the subject of work by Bika (1997). Her work extols the virtues of expanding the school space into opportunities for constructive engagement. She explains the historical movement toward "new schools," which had, as a fundamental element, the concept of physical location beyond the city so that children would learn to work with their hands, and connect the real world with the symbolic world of school. We can create that environment within our schools by attending to the choice of objects in the classroom, and to the dimensions of space that can be created by moving furniture, establishing zones for particular types of activities; in effect, we can turn a classroom into a learning studio.

When we break the habits and patterns that dictate what a classroom should look like, we can create an environment that challenges thinking. Imagine your classroom as an art studio, a television stage set, an aquarium, a forest, another planet. Create the environment that will set the stage for the lessons in all subjects, supported by the creative arts. Giving children the opportunity to create their own learning space is effective in giving them ownership in the education process. A sense of space can be created within a classroom as well as beyond it, and unforgettable learning can happen there, too.

References

Bika, A. (1997, September). *A system for the expansion and development of school into a space of constructive engagement for childhood age categories.* Paper presented at the European Conference on the Quality of Early Childhood Education, Munich, Germany. (ERIC Document Reproduction Service No. ED 438053)

Franck, F. (1979). *The awakened eye.* New York: Vintage Books/Random House.

Gordon, W. J. J., & Poze, T. (1972). *Strange & familiar.* Boston: Synectics Education Systems.

Loughran, S. (2001). An artist among young artists: A lesson for teachers. *Childhood Education, 77,* 201-208.

Moore, R. C., & Wong, H. H. (1997). *Natural learning: Creating environments for rediscovering nature's way of teaching.* Berkeley, CA: MIG Communications.

Mueller, F. L. (1993, December). *Phototext authoring: Embracing diversity in the classroom.* Paper and activity presentation at the 1993 National Staff Development Council Annual Conference, Dallas, TX.

Piaget, J. (1955). *The language and thought of the child.* Cleveland, OH: World Publishing.

Rasmusen, H., & Grant, A. (1967). *Sculpture from junk.* New York: Reinhold Publishing.

Ruggiero, J. (1981). *Found objects: A style and source book* (pp. xi-xiv). New York: Clarkson N. Potter.

Slesin, S. (1981). Introduction. In J. Ruggiero (Ed.), *Found objects: A style and source book.* New York: Clarkson N. Potter.

Stribling, M. L. (1970). *Art from found materials: Discarded and natural.* New York: Crown.

CHAPTER 15

Geography
Fieldwork and Curriculum in the Out-of-Doors

Judith C. Mimbs, Douglas Heffington, and Lisa Herring-Mayo

Judith C. Mimbs is a teacher at Soddy Daisy High School, Soddy Daisy, Tennessee.
Douglas Heffington is a professor at Middle Tennessee State University,
Murfreesboro, Tennessee. Lisa Herring-Mayo is a world geography teacher at
Warren County High School, in McMinnville, Tennessee, and an instructor
at Williamson Christian College, Franklin, Tennessee.

The cornerstone of geography is considered by many to be based on fieldwork and field observation, the most primary of geography's laboratories. However, fieldwork in the K-8 curriculum is seldom addressed and even more infrequently incorporated into the classroom. A strong background in field observation and geographic fieldwork may provide a logical outlet for better understanding the world, how it is organized spatially, and how geography can best address the essential elements and standards for achieving those goals. Students engaging in simple, straightforward, relevant, and fun-filled activities relating to the National Geography Standards are more likely to apply this newfound knowledge and geographical insight to their lives (National Geographic Society, 1994).

It has been proposed by Goodlad (1984) and others that teacher training take the form of medical school training, with students learning theory and putting that into practice to see what does and does not work, and why. The same can be applied to school children. If students put their knowledge into practice, they will learn from the experience. What better place to practice geography than outdoors? This experience can begin in the early grades and continue through high school.

Geography and the Out-of-Doors

Outdoor classroom activities provide opportunities for students to view environmental relationships that are difficult to explain within a traditional classroom setting. Outdoor classroom activities may lead to improvement of long-term retention of basic and complex environmental concepts. Davis Kaila, president of Celemi, Inc., a pioneer in the creation of business simulations (primary tools in experiential learning), cites a number of research projects that demonstrate the retention rate of passive classroom learning is only 20 percent, while the retention rate of experiential learners is 90 percent. Fieldwork, the major component of out-of-doors geography, "give(s) opportunities for learning which cannot be duplicated in the classroom. It greatly enhances students' understanding of geographical features and concepts, and allows students to develop specific as well as general skills" (Her Majesty's Inspectors, 1992, p. 1).

Outdoor education long has been considered a viable, practicable approach to science education. Yet its direct applications to the field of geography have, more often than not, been ignored. Upon close examination of the research in geography, it becomes apparent that the foundations of the discipline itself lie in field observations, those fundamental sources of *primary* data.

Research has suggested that field-oriented instruction is popular for several reasons, one being that the content cannot be reproduced in traditional classroom settings. The processes of learning are enhanced by field-oriented study, because students are brought into direct, firsthand contact with the object(s) under investigation. The instructor's role focuses less on lecturing and more on facilitating and guiding students in their endeavors to discover, analyze, and interpret. Improved learning performance and heightened environmental consciousness are also inextricably tied to field-oriented instruction. Kern and Carpenter (1984) suggest that fieldwork has a role as a vehicle for integrating and illustrating theoretical concepts, and is particularly effective in fostering student understanding of abstract topics and higher level concepts, which are easier to teach in the field than in the classroom. In many cases, students experience more interest, enjoyment, and academic accomplishment in field settings than in traditional lecture/classroom courses. The challenge is to successfully incorporate traditional and unconventional methods of learning into cohesive, complementary elements which, if effectively united, maximize any student's learning potential.

According to Beirsdorfer and Davis (1994), field-oriented courses provide an excellent venue for collaborative projects. Students often engage in more creative discussions and produce more original, higher quality work than they do in traditional courses. Field-oriented courses also may improve such team skills as leadership, task management, and effective communication. Such courses also may generate more enthusiasm, collaboration, and effort among team members.

Mackenzie and White (1982) found that field-oriented instruction benefited students' understanding and long-term retention of targeted concepts while conducting their research. Students' performances on assessments related to their fieldwork also demonstrated strong retention levels, showing improvement in conceptualization of the materials.

Fieldwork is essential in any geography curriculum. Knowledge of geography is gained by direct observation. Work in the field is the best way to gather and understand geographic knowledge. The art of field observation "is an acquired skill and can be honed every time students examine the world around them" (Heffington, 1997, p. 73). The "field" can be defined as any place where "supervised learning can take place via first-hand experience, outside the constraints of the four-wall classroom setting" (Lonergan & Anderson, 1988, p. 64).

The following field exercise, in lesson plan format, involves students' understanding of basic cardinal directions and how to use them while identifying the physical and human characteristics of their school playground(s), in the guise of a treasure hunt. It is an exercise meant to take them into the field where geographic concepts can be applied to the learning experience. After all, places and regions are the basic units of geography, and different people see them in different ways. Places and Regions, one of the six essential elements dividing the subject matter of geography into comprehensive units, epitomizes the organization of geographic information, as demonstrated in the exercise. The identities of individuals and peoples are rooted in particular places, as well as in the human constructs called regions. Our "sense of self" is, indeed, bound to our "sense of place." Who we are is sometimes indistinguishable from where we are; to better understand other peoples, cultures, and regions of the world, it is important for students to understand their own places.

Playground Places

The following field exercise represents one way that necessary and important geographic knowledge and skills might be developed in elementary students. This lesson plan affords elementary students the opportunity to learn the foundations of directions and to identify the physical and human characteristics of their school's surroundings.

Purpose: To learn about directions on maps and how to use the directions when reading maps.

Title: Playground Places.

Geography Standards: I. The World in Spatial Terms: How to use maps and other geographical representations to acquire, process, and report information from a spatial perspective; and IV. Places and Regions: Physical and human characteristics of places.

Objectives:

- Be introduced to field observation methods and map-making
- Demonstrate proficient skill in determining the differences in the basic directions of left, right, front, and back
- Demonstrate knowledge of the link between basic directions and cardinal directions of north, south, east, and west
- Be introduced to the compass and learn how to orient oneself by using the device
- Conduct meaningful field observations in a designated playground area as student first verbalizes, then draws, the physical and cultural characteristics of the field observation area.

Materials:

- Adult volunteers will be needed for hiding treasures and map help
- Several different styles of maps, both physical and cultural, large- and small-scale
- Transparency of a compass
- Class set of real compasses

Set: Ask students whether any one of them knows what a map is. Ask for reasons maps might be used or needed. Ask them to think about why maps are made, then explain that maps are based on directions and observations. Explain that compasses are devices that are used to show people how to find their way around places, using basic directions. Show a transparency of a compass and illustrate the directions (students may be asked to hold their hands out with only their "pointer" fingers and thumbs extended, with the teacher explaining that the hands whose fingers make the shape of an "L" are the left, or west hands, which may be helpful when the exercise in directions begins). Tell students that they will be using their compasses to create maps of their playground and school building(s).

Procedures:

1. Explain how the compass works and what a map's compass rose is.

2. Divide the students into groups of three or four. Have each group take a small object, hereafter known as a "treasure," from a box, without letting any other group see it. The group will show its object to the teacher only, and it will be recorded. Explain that each group will hide its treasure somewhere on the playground, and only they and the adults will know what the "treasure" is and where it is hidden. It is the task of the treasure "hunters" in another group to find the objects, using the maps the "hiders" will draw and provide.

3. Divide the students into groups, instructing each group to draw a map of the playground, paying attention to the directional readings on their compasses as they draw the features of the area, such as the swing sets, the slide, the monkey bars, etc. Ask them to include the compass roses on their maps. Once completed, have each group go outside with a volunteer to hide its treasure. When the group comes back, have the volunteer tell the teacher where the treasure was hidden, so you will be able to assist them with writing basic directions to the treasure on the maps they have already drawn. This process should be repeated until all of the treasures have been hidden and all of the map directions are completed. The teacher and volunteers then will have the groups swap maps and the treasure hunt will begin.

Designate a home base from which each group will start the hunt, and to which each group will return with their found treasure. Explain that each group should use its map to hunt for the treasure and, when it is found, they should return to home base to show it to the teacher.

Evaluation: Students will be evaluated in two ways:

1. Was each group able to create a simple map with basic directions, including a compass rose, with physical playground objects included for reference?

2. Were groups able to follow the directions and find the treasures?

Extension: Ask another classroom group to participate in a treasure hunt, using the maps your students produced.

Examples of Fieldwork Activities That Address the National Geography Standards

The World in Spatial Terms
- Sketch maps
- Follow directions
- Analyze different types of maps of a local area before, during, and after fieldwork

Places and Regions
- Examine characteristics of places
- Identify what humans do
- Compare one's own locality with other localities

Physical Systems
- Identify features of landscapes
- Examine weather and season characteristics
- Find out where water comes from and how it is used

Human Systems
- Where people live and why
- Why people move from place to place
- How humans use buildings

Environment and Society
- Human influences on the environment
- Identify places that can be polluted and how to protect them

The Uses of Geography
- Identify different points of view that can affect development, as well as policies to manage resources
- Identify local problems
- A geographical dimension, and possible solutions

(Sources: *Geography for Life,* 1994; Rice & Bulman, 2001)

Conclusions

If students put their knowledge into practice, they will learn from the experience. What better place to practice geography than outdoors? This experience can begin in the elementary grades and continue through high school (Mimbs, 2002).

Outdoor classroom activities provide opportunities for students to view environmental relationships that are difficult to explain within a traditional classroom setting. Outdoor classroom activities may lead to improved long-term retention of basic and complex environmental concepts.

References

Beirsdorfer, R. A., & Davis, W. E. (1994). Suggestions for planning a class field trip. *Journal of College Science Teaching, 23,* 302-311.

Goodlad, J. (1984). *A place called school.* New York: McGraw-Hill.

Heffington, J. D. (1997). Ethnicity: Lessons from the field. In L. E. Estaville & C. J. Rosen (Eds.), *Teaching American ethnic geography. Pathways in Geography Series Title No. 18* (pp. 79-89). Jacksonville, AL: National Council for Geographic Education.

Her Majesty's Inspectors. (1992). *A survey of geography fieldwork in degree courses: A report by HMI.* Stanmore, Middlesex, England: Author.

Inner, A. M. (1986). *Geography starts here!* Sheffield, UK: The Geographical Association.

Kern, E., & Carpenter, J. (1984). Enhancement of student values, interests, and attitudes in earth science through a field-oriented approach. *Journal of Geological Education, 21,* 299-305.

Lonergan, N., & Anderson, L. W. (1988). Field-based education: Some theoretical considerations. *Higher Education Research and Development, 7,* 63-77.

Mackenzie, A., & White, R. (1982). Fieldwork in geography and long-term memory structures. *American Education Research Journal, 19,* 623-632.

Mimbs, J. C. (2002). *Geography education requirements in K-8 preservice teacher training at southern regional education board colleges and universities and development of a field-oriented model curriculum.* Doctoral dissertation, University of Tennessee, Knoxville.

National Geographic Society. (1994). *Geography for life: The national geography standards.* Washington, DC: Author.

Rice, G. A., & Bulman, T. L. (2001). *Fieldwork-1 in the Geography Curriculum: Filling the Rhetoric-reality.* National Council for Geographic Education, Indiana University of Pennsylvania, Indiana, PA.

www.nationalgeographic.com

www.ngs.org

The Out-of- Doors and Our Future

Kathleen G. Burriss and Barbara Foulks Boyd

Some futurists look ahead and see our descendents living in underground habitats or encased in above-ground glass and metal shells. But why? Often, these scenarios follow speculation of a global catastrophe. Yet our future may be devoid of the out-of-doors without such a catastrophe, simply because of its inconvenience or our lack of connectedness. Historically, incorporating the out-of-doors environment has been integral to the human experience. The history of humankind represents the ongoing adaptation of people and the environment—to initiate exploration, mediate challenge, and accommodate variation. The challenge of the out-of-doors has served to both provoke and soothe human evolution. That is, the outdoor experience enables men and women to develop cognitive, social, emotional, and physical prowess otherwise unavailable. Current societal trends undermine children's opportunities to naturally engage the out-of-door environment and, thereby, threaten the tenuous balance between people and their outdoor environments.

Recently, society appears to be moving toward more structured and controlled living patterns. While the technologically based workplace is convenient, it leads adults to a nonphysical lifestyle. Parents spend long hours at the workplace. Adults spend a lot of money to join gyms, where natural exercise is re-created by walking on treadmills, lifting weights, or using rowing machines. And what of the children?

Children, after similarly long, sedentary school days, frequently arrive home before their parents do. Their ability to play in the neighborhood is often restricted by the late hour, limited adult supervision, or lack of defined, safe playscapes. Children's days and weekends are filled with lessons, activities, and organized sports events. What this contrived lifestyle holds for the development of future generations is not clear. Despite the abundant research extolling the benefits of free play for children's social, emotional, cognitive, and physical development, fewer children can be found enjoying playtime in neighborhoods, parks, or community playgrounds. Opportunities for children to choose their playscape are decreasing. The reasons given for closely monitoring children's playtime include parents' work schedules, lack of trained supervision, and concern for safety. Instead of going home after school to skate on a neighbor's home-made rink, build a clubhouse in the field, or meet a group to play ball, children attend after-school programs, sports activities, and classes like karate and ballet. While there is nothing inherently wrong with these structured activities, they cannot replace the developmental contributions of free-choice outdoor play.

While new millennium children may be technologically savvy, they are still children and need to engage their interest and learning outside. To do otherwise is to deny them opportunities to connect with their human history by exploring and adapting to the out-of-doors. At the same time, the ability of children to play out-of-doors in order to relieve stress, develop self-esteem, and construct meaning of the physical world diminishes.

Traditionally, school activities have provided access to outdoor learning and play, but this role, too, is threatened. The academic pressure for higher test scores causes outdoor learning and play to be viewed as superfluous to "real" school learning. Going out-of-doors is often regarded as a privilege that children must earn during the school day and enjoy after their "real schoolwork" is completed. Recess and other outdoor pursuits provide children with valuable social, emotional, and intellectual learning, in addition to physical development. Whether it is for recess, a walk, or to read a story, children look forward to their time outside. Out-of-door activities are a crucial part of elementary learning and development, and children have a right to engage in them. An alarming number of school districts throughout the United States have decreased, and in some cases eliminated, outside time for elementary-age children.

The current notion is that children have enough time to play outside after regular school hours. However, this is not the case. The time children spend with peers outside is different from inside play and learning, and it provides singularly unique opportunities for learning. While few dispute the benefits for physical development, the bountiful social, emotional, and intellectual learning opportunities to be found out-of-doors also must be acknowledged and valued.

The outside is a place of aesthetics, calm, and wonder. These are not attributes an educator can teach directly; rather, time and varied experiences nurture children's appreciation. In this technological era as children drill for tests and press for academic gains, we may, as a culture, lose irretrievable benefits if out-of-doors play and learning are not legitimized. The choices we make today will determine our tomorrow. And what choice will we make?